CW00816180

# THE RIVER PRINCE

# THE RIVER PRINCE

*by*

CHRIS YATES

2009
THE MEDLAR PRESS
ELLESMERE

Published by The Medlar Press Limited,
The Grange, Ellesmere, Shropshire SY12 9DE
www.medlarpress.com

ISBN 978-1-899600-65-6
First published as a limited edition 1998
This edition published 2009



Designed and typeset in 11½ on 14pt Bembo Roman.

Produced in England by The Medlar Press Limited,
Ellesmere, England.

*'The barbel, than which*
*fish a braver doth not swim.'*

Michael Drayton

# *Contents*

## *Introduction*

I had been fishing for twenty-three years before I made my first cast for a barbel. It was a revelation. It was a whole new dimension. Barbel fishing! It was such fun, and such a welcome contrast to my carp fishing which had, over the previous few years, become rather serious and over intense.

I had only recently landed my record carp from Redmire and, because of the interest that fish aroused, it seemed to me that the whole world had become focused on carp fishing. It was, therefore, a ripe moment for me to discover a new branch of angling.

After the deep stillness of a carp pool, a barbel stream seemed so lively and vital - positively conversational. And even though I was a carp stalker rather than a carp trapper, barbel fishing was a far more active pursuit. The barbel themselves were certainly as powerful as carp, but more elegant and definitely more enigmatic.

Such was my total enthusiasm for all things barbelish I think I was in danger of becoming just as obsessive as I had been about carp, but now, after sixteen years, I've got my equilibrium back again: I'm a more broad minded, catholic angler, though I probably still love barbel too much.

Like most fishermen, I have always enjoyed reading about my favourite species and this book reflects my passion, though it is a result, really, of my earlier obsession, when I used to scour every library and bookshop in search of barbel stories. It was soon apparent that, compared to all the other major species, there was only a very limited amount of *barbus* literature. And this made the fish and the writing seem even more appealing.

There is a whole sea of salmon fishing stories, a whole river of trout tales and an oceanic lake of carp fables. But for the barbel there is - or was - just a short winding stream with a few deep pools.

Nowadays, this lack of barbel fishing writing has at least been acknowledged and there are certainly more books on the subject than there were ten years ago, but, apart from one or two exceptions, none of the writing is in quite the same class as the few earlier classics. That is why I include pieces which are mostly from the golden era of angling writing and very little recent material. There are, I realise, some fascinating stories from contemporary barbel anglers, especially the unbelievable tale by Dave Williams of his three fourteen-pounders, but perhaps I could persuade the publisher to include these in a second companion to this edition.

I have included a recent short piece of my own, not because I think it stands comparison with the classics, but simply because it shows where I am now with my barbel fishing. And I have also persuaded John Ginifer to finally set down one of the most extraordinary stories in barbel angling history, 'Walking Away from the Thames' - a story that Sheringham and Ransome would have loved.

*Chris Yates, October 1998*

## The Avon at Ibsley

*Chris Yates*

A great cumulus boiled over the valley at tea-time. The sun went in a few minutes later and, almost instantly, it began to rain - first a gentle pattering, then something more intense: the most significant downpour for a month, darkening the soil, congealing the dust, knocking the leaves off the beech trees and sprouting the image in my head that always flowers with the first real deluge of autumn.

In summer I'm a carp fisher and the image in my head is nearly a hundred per cent carp, only occasionally shape-shifting to become tench, or rudd; but when the autumn rains come, and the autumn smells, I can only think about barbel.

I knew Mick was on the Avon at Ibsley. But I'd said, when he phoned yesterday, that I'd only 'probably' see him there. It wasn't barbel weather yesterday - though Mick had obviously sensed it would be, despite the confidently summery weather forecast. As soon as the rain set in I knew I'd have to go and find him and perhaps share a fish or two with him, if I was lucky. He was almost exactly where I had guessed he'd be; down by the stile at the Deepening. The light was grey and poor and the rain, though lessening, was still veiling anything further than quarter of a mile. But even as I came across the wide field towards the river I could recognise the figure standing next to the trees by the daft little businessman's brolly he was holding. Within fifty yards I could also see a distinctive plume of pipe smoke. He slowly turned when I finally reached him and by his expression I knew he'd had a good day.

"Three," he said in answer to my question. "A five-pounder, a six and an eight. Isn't this weather wonderful!" The river was still quite clear and low, but there was a fair amount of jetsam coming down in the form of dead leaves and bits of weed.

"It's just beginning to rise now," said Mick. "And it's not as clear as it was this morning."

As he spoke a fish porpoised in the main pool. I didn't see it clearly, but I caught the unmistakable gold flash as it turned on the surface.

"I think I'd better cast a line," I said.

I went upstream into the copse at the top of the pool, where the main flow crosses diagonally from the near to the far bank. Putting together a light eleven-foot two-piece, centrepin and six-pound line, I squelched through a reed-bed and cast. With no more than a little flick of the rod the bait was trundling nicely away and down, then checked to be swung out of the current, into the quiet back flow below me - to my right. I let it infuse there for a few minutes, but nothing was drawn towards the sweet fragrance of bacon grill. Casting again, I noticed the rain had stopped, the clouds were lifting and the whole riverscape was steaming in the suddenly cooler evening air. The ideal ingredients, I thought - after rain, light fading, soft mist - mixing perfectly to form the image I was looking for.

I smelt pipe smoke drifting invisibly from upstream. Mick had obviously moved swims and was now somewhere above the copse. I'd just heard the distant plop of his bait when my rod top curved decisively over and - yes - it wasn't a jagging chub - yes - it wasn't a swaying eel - yes - it was an almost indifferent, depth-holding barbel. It eventually realised that I was disturbing it and drove down and away, getting around the midstream weed-bed, jamming me. With the cane bent to the butt, I eased the fish back, inch by inch, and gradually worked it to my side of the weeds. A tail slapped the surface, disappeared again and once more the Aerial sang my favourite song. I shouted over the top of it and heard Mick's distant "coming!" I'd need a hand with the net, what with the extensive rooted raft of mint and bogbean right in front of me.

The barbel surfaced again and lounged there, looking quite large. Mick appeared through the trees behind me, picked up the net, but passed it straight to me when he saw the depth of the situation. He was not equipped to wade: one more step and his shoes would have filled with mud and water. I had to coax the fish all the way round to the lower end of the mint and bean raft before I could reach it. In knee length boots, I still got a wet right foot, though I didn't notice till later. The barbel curved nicely into the mesh and with a mass of clinging weed and a burst of spray, I heaved it up, swung it round and laid it gently amongst the bankside reeds.

Because the clouds were breaking, the evening had a tinge of blue about it, yet it was all like ash against a fish that glowed bright as a molten ingot. I ran a finger along the fine gold scales and could see the silhouettes of both Mick and myself in the gold rimmed eye. "Lovely fish," said Mick.

"Eight pounds?" I said, not that it mattered.

"Certainly."

Autumn was always bonfire smoke, Cox's apples, fallen leaves, hazelnuts, conkers - but for me it will also be the elegant barbel, who is at his prime at this season. I let his image burn into my head even as I gave it back to the river.

# The Middle Avon

*Dick Walker*

Ever since barbel were introduced into the Dorset Stour and found their way from that river into the Hampshire Avon, the latter river has been famous for producing very large specimens, which include two out of the three 14 lb 6 oz fish that share the record at the time of writing. Both these fish came from the fabulous Royalty Fisheries at Christchurch, and even larger barbel have been found dead, or caught out of season by salmon anglers in this stretch of the river.

Barbel, however, are not confined to the Royalty Fisheries - they inhabit the river at least as far upstream as Downton in Wiltshire. It is in fact possible to catch a fish far exceeding the present record, anywhere between that town and the tide limit at Christchurch.

The behaviour of the barbel above the Royalty is quite different from that of fish in the Royalty. Many of the fish are huge, fish of 16 and 17 lb having been caught accidentally by salmon anglers between Ibsley and Sopley either by foulhooking or out of season. Even bigger fish have been seen by anglers well qualified to judge the weights, and I am in no doubt whatsoever about the existence of 20 lb fish, because I myself have also seen them, when other anglers like Fred J. Taylor, Peter Thomas and Colonel Crow have been present and agreed to the estimated size.

Except at spawning time when they form shoals of anything up to fifty or sixty fish, these middle Avon barbel are in small groups which become smaller and smaller as the season progresses. The greatest number I ever saw together in the coarse fishing season was twelve, half of them over the record. That was on the first day of July, 1964. Within a couple of weeks only two or three barbel remained in the swim.

The shoals seem to disperse gradually after spawning. By June 16th they are down to a dozen or so fish and by the end of July they are in two's and three's with many solitary specimens. These small groups, and individual fish, are spread over a very great length of the river, because the barbel population in these middle reaches is far, far less than it is in the Royalty Fisheries.

It is, therefore, very difficult to locate the fish, and the situation is further complicated by the fact that a great deal of wandering about by groups and individuals takes place. Even if the angler locates a group of two or three fish, the probability is that they will have moved elsewhere by the following day. By noticing fish that can be recognised by marks of one kind or another, it can be stated that it is not unusual for them to move as much as half a mile from one day to the next.

It may be that this tendency on the part of barbel, and the bigger specimens in particular, is due to the savage and indiscriminate weed-cutting that is now done regularly by the River Authority, when every particle of weed that the cutters can reach is removed. The extensive use of crop sprays may also play its part, but whatever the reason, contrary to popular belief, the middle Avon is far from rich in molluscs, crustacea and insect life. I say this after very extensive examination of what little weed remains after cutting, of the second growth of weed in late summer, and the river-bed itself. There is an extensive population of freshwater shrimp *(gammarus pulex)* in weed that has survived the cutting and among the larger stones where the current is moderate. On the larger stones in fast water there are colonies of a sedge larvae with an adherent caddis case, which, I believe, is the larvae of the grey flag sedge. Other organisms, thought existent in considerable variety, are not present in large quantities and I have a theory, as yet unproven, that a substantial part of the food of the barbel is obtained from the simple algae that grows on the stones and river-bed gravel. Removal of the rooted weed allows much more light to reach these stones and a profuse growth of algae results. It is common on the middle Avon in summertime to find irregular patches of clean stones on the bottom of the river and I think it is at least possible that barbel are responsible.

So, the angler has a difficult enough problem in locating the barbel and deciding how and when to fish for them. It is made even more difficult by the presence of other fish. There are a very large number of dace, a considerable population of chub, plenty of eels, brown trout, salmon parr, and in some areas perch and roach. No bait attractive to barbel is immune from the attentions of other species, which outnumber the barbel with a ratio of many thousands to one.

The combination of all these factors makes a deliberate capture of a middle Avon barbel the most difficult problem I have ever attempted to solve. Discounting small fish, I have succeeded in some seven or eight years in catching three of them - a 12 lb 12 oz specimen and two 9 lb fish. On the Royalty I have had a 12-pounder, an 11-pounder and two 9-pounders in a couple of hours. This may give some idea of the difference between barbel fishing in the Royalty and the rest of the Hampshire Avon.

Despite the lack of success, however, some useful speculation is possible. Up to 1962 the Throop fishery on the Stour, though containing many more barbel than a comparable stretch of the middle Avon, yielded very few barbel. By comparison with the Royalty, little fishing was done at Throop and very little of that was for barbel, but from 1962 onwards, the overcrowding on the Royalty Fisheries combined with an increase in the number of anglers having their own transport, has resulted in far more people fishing the Stour. Since that time barbel catches have increased enormously and by a far greater extent than the increase in the number of anglers fishing. It is difficult to draw any conclusions other than that the bait thrown in by anglers, hempseed, maggots, cheese, and bread, have now reached the quantity where the barbel regard them as part of the natural diet, which has been the case on the Royalty Fisheries for a great number of years. It seems likely that barbel, and especially big barbel, fail to recognise as food any material that is not fairly regularly available as food in considerable quantities. This may explain why the middle Avon barbel regularly refuse any of the baits we offer them, even when we can positively locate the fish and put a bait right in front of their noses without scaring them.

All the barbel I have caught on the middle Avon, with one exception, were caught on maggots after a long session of feeding a great many maggots into the swim I was fishing. Like many other anglers on this part of the river I have hooked and lost big barbel on fine tackle while roach fishing, using big quantities of maggots fed continuously down the swim.

Very similar considerations probably apply to the Great Ouse, which holds far more barbel than is generally supposed. Very few anglers indeed ever fish for them, and when one is hooked by an angler after roach, bream or dace with fine tackle, it is practically certain to escape, usually without the angler ever discovering what sort of fish was responsible. On the middle Avon the same kind of devastating breaks are often attributed to salmon, which, despite what books written by salmon anglers may say, are often quite willing to take not only worm baits, but maggots, bread, or cheese. I have even known one attack an angler's float. Of course salmon very often are responsible for breakages, but many times a break is likely to be caused by big barbel. Salmon anglers, of course, catch barbel. Some of these are foulhooked, which is not surprising when one considers how methodically a good salmon angler covers a pool with a devon, complete with treble hooks, spun a few inches off the bottom, but there is little doubt that some of the barbel which salmon anglers catch, quite deliberately attack the lure. They have been hooked well inside the mouth. On the Avon, salmon fishing begins in February and continues legally until October, but for practical purposes finishes about the end of June. The accidental capture of barbel on spinners appears to take place between March and April for the most part. I do not wish to imply that large numbers of barbel are taken by salmon anglers, but it is probably at least as many, if we consider only double-figure fish, as the coarse fish angler catches. From this one might deduce that a small fish, dead or alive would make a useful bait for big barbel, but this has not proved the case in the coarse fish season. Visible barbel have positively refused such offerings, but eels, chub, and small pike have not! It seems unlikely that big barbel would prefer metal or wooden devons to real fish, but even if they did, the terms upon which coarse fishing is permitted on the middle Avon seldom includes the use of salmon spinning tackle.

My record of failure to catch these great fish makes me ill-qualified to offer advice about catching them, but for what it is worth, here is what I suggest. Try to locate the fish, and don't consider a whole day too long to devote to searching for them. The hook should be baited with a sample of whatever you have chosen for groundbait, and the tackle should be strong enough to give you a fair chance if you hook a record fish. I would not be happy with anything less than 6 lb line or a hook smaller than a size 8.

I know big barbel are caught in the Royalty Fishery with much finer tackle, for I've caught them myself, but these are fish which have been hooked, played and landed many times. A big, fit, middle Avon barbel is a very different proposition.

Most middle Avon swims shallow off at the downstream end and as dusk approaches, the angler should work his bait into shallower water. The choice of whether to use leger or float tackle must depend on the nature of the swim chosen, but long hours of fishing are often involved, ending in darkness, so most of the fishing is done with a leger rig.

I have had too few bites to advise about their pattern. On other waters the bite from a barbel may be a tremble, a rattle on the rod-tip, or a solid, thumping pull. All my middle Avon barbel have been of the last type.

Of course there will be no lack of bites from other species when fishing a middle Avon barbel swim and the angler has to bear this philosophically, frequently replacing the chewed up worm, the sucked out maggot skins, the missing flake, crust, or cheese. He must expect to catch numerous chub, eels, dace and trout. He will probably be amazed to find that an Avon dace weighing a bare ounce, can hook itself on a No. 4 hook baited with a big worm.

Often he will have to choose a swim that he is not sure holds barbel at all, because after a long tiring walk along many miles of the river bank he has failed to see a single barbel. Even when he does find a few he will not be certain that they are still there after an hour of fishing. He must be prepared to fish on as if a 20 lb barbel was about to bite in the next few seconds, and he must keep at it, not only hour after hour but day after day, month after month, season after season, if he is really determined to get to grips with one of the monsters.

Once he has seen a few of them, however, he will be supported by the hope that one day, perhaps within a few minutes, perhaps in a few years, there will come that pull, made with the power and authority that distinguishes a barbel bite from that of any other fish, which will tell him that if he does everything right, he may make angling history.

# The House Pool

*Fred J. Taylor*

I do not know if the practice of baiting weir pools with thousands of lobworms encased in balls of clay for a week before fishing is still practised today, but I do know that it is certainly not practised as often or as widely as it was over half a century ago.

Although I wasn't fishing half a century ago, I know anglers who were, and I have read everything I can find about barbel fishing. I have fished with the modern experts and I have discussed it with the older exponents of the art, men who have caught more barbel than I am ever likely to, and it seems that times have changed.

However, I wonder if the old methods would be successful today if they were practised as seriously as they used to be? Are the barbel today still in the same places, in such large numbers or are they more widely distributed? How would they react today to the heavy groundbaitings with greaves which they used to encounter in the old days? I do not know whether the barbel's taste has altered during the passing years or if modern baits have educated the barbel into accepting something different, but it does seem to me that barbel baits of the past are losing favour. Techniques, too, are different and undoubtedly the barbel is being sought in different places. One never hears of the huge bags of barbel which used to be taken in one day's fishing on some of the better known Thames weir pools; and nowadays half a dozen barbel is considered a fine catch.

There will always be recognised barbel swims of course; swims which one only has to look at and say without doubt that they will contain barbel. There will always be barbel in weir pools but they are also turning up nowadays in sluggish sidestreams and backwaters which one would not normally consider to be suitable for barbel. Some of the barbel in these minor waters are huge and could well be record breakers if caught, but the fishing for them is so vastly different to what used to be considered orthodox barbel fishing. I have seen and caught barbel from waters less than two feet deep in what can only be described as a 'brook'. Some of them have been very big, others only small but I have never managed to catch more than one at a time.

Barbel in such waters do not respond to groundbaiting because they appear to be travellers and are seldom in the same place two days running. They are either 'at home' or not, and if they are 'at home' they may or may not feed. If they are disinclined to feed, all the groundbait in the world will not induce them to begin. At times they occupy what are commonly called 'barbel holes' and while it is quite true that they *are* barbel holes they certainly cannot be described as 'barbel *feeding* holes'. What seems to happen is that they emerge from these holes either at dawn or approaching dusk and begin to feed either on the edge of the hole, or more often, actually in the shallows which invariably run into it. If it was possible to extract a barbel without making any noise or disturbance I am sure that moderate bags could be taken but, as it is, the landing of one fish promptly causes the others to retreat.

Various methods and baits have been tried in order to catch these barbel, ranging from ordinary bread crust to lumps of sausage meat, and all have been successful from time to time, with the exception of lobworms. This doesn't prove anything, of course, because it may just mean that barbel and lobworm were not in the same place at the same time! I wonder, however, what Francis Francis or Philip Geen would think if they were alive today, and could see an angler casting half a pork sausage into a muddy sidestream about two feet deep in the hope of catching a large barbel! The truth is of course that the angler of today may not catch as many barbel as Francis Francis but he will certainly have the chance to catch one a lot bigger.

Barbel and their tastes vary from water to water as they appear to have done from century to century, and while it is still possible to catch barbel on lobworms from a variety of waters it does seem that lobworms are losing favour and that cheese in one form or another is taking its place. Barbel in the Hampshire Avon have a decided liking for cheese and more recently there has been a preference for the Dutch cheese. Kennet barbel prefer a softer cheese and any of the many processed varieties will take them, as will also a soft cheese paste.

The Kennet is in many respects a miniature Avon and, although I do not know the Avon very well, it seems that the methods of fishing both rivers are somewhat similar. The tendency to anchor one's bait in the current has lessened considerably and now the general practice is to allow the bait to roll downstream until it settles under the streamer weed. It has been found that with lighter leads and finer lines the likelihood of the tackle becoming snagged or the bait becoming obscured is less than with a heavy outfit. Barbel are strong fish but they do not often bolt into weed immediately they are hooked as do the chub or carp, and there is a good chance of their being landed even on very fine gear.

It may be said of cheese and cheese paste that the only reason for the barbel's interest is the fact that cheese has been introduced into the river in large quantities and that the barbel have become accustomed to finding it there. But I wonder if this is the case. Surely no one could say, of the Thames backwaters already mentioned, that the barbel had become accustomed to finding sausages there! The price of sausages is such that one would seldom take more than a couple of pounds for a day's fishing, although I know one angler who baited a swim with seven pounds on one occasion. "They were beef," he said, "pork would make the barbel feel important." Looking back though, I wonder how much difference there is, to a barbel, between chandler's greaves and modern sausages!

Two other baits which have been successful over the past few years are crayfish and freshwater mussel, but this is probably because modern anglers have *used* these baits. It is doubtful if the old exponents did. I can understand any large fish learning that a crayfish is good to eat and it is logical to expect a barbel to accept a crayfish presented naturally. Mussels, however, have a very tough shell and I cannot imagine how a barbel can learn that the *inside* of a mussel is good to eat. When using mussels as bait for tench and other stillwater fish I have always found it necessary to pre-bait an area with mussel flesh before the fish have accepted them. Barbel in certain minor waters, however, have been known to accept them without any preliminaries. I have never known *any* fish take mussels where they did not exist naturally, however, and I have no doubt that the fish knew all about mussels before anglers tried to teach them.

There are probably a lot more barbel caught today than there were a hundred years ago, but there are also a lot more anglers fishing for them. We shall probably not catch them in hundredweights like our ancestors did because we shall be unable to pursue them in the same manner. The days when the countryman was glad to earn a few shillings collecting lobworms and baiting swims for the gentry have passed, and our barbel fishing is no longer dependent upon someone else's poverty. One fine example of the great difference in techniques practised today may be found in the swim known locally as the 'House Pool'. It is situated at the upstream end of a Thames feeder stream in Oxfordshire and is adjacent to the gardens of a row of houses. Opposite are other houses and downstream on either side are playing fields. Children play 'ducks and drakes' and float toy boats in the swim. They also play football on the banks and, if fish are scared by such carryings-on, the fish in the House Pool ought to be terrified. Terrified or not, however, they are still caught occasionally and, although this chapter is mainly devoted to the barbel therein, a brief mention of some of the other fish may be of interest.

It contains perhaps all of the more common coarse fish and many specimens have been taken. It is quite a fabulous pool and as well as large numbers of barbel, specimen roach, chub, bream and pike have been taken there from time to time. Several chub over five pounds and one weighing a little over six pounds have been caught. Roach over two pounds are sometimes caught and one weighing 2 lb 10 oz was taken a few years ago. Occasionally a bream puts in an appearance, and several over five pounds have fallen to barbel fishermen. The most common occurrence when fishing the House Pool, however, is to come away biteless or, alternatively, exasperated after striking at nibbling dace all day and failing to hook one. This is not the swim for the casual fisherman who likes to watch a stationary float, or to trot a fine tackle downstream. It is *not* a pleasant spot as far as nature's beauties are concerned and one's attention will never be distracted by sight of a kingfisher, the sunset, or by the dawn chorus. Floating debris from allotments upstream is continually floating down with the current, giving false registration on the rod tip as it fouls the line in passing.

The only attraction as far as I am concerned is the fact that it holds double-figure barbel and specimen fish of other kinds, and I am prepared to put up with its faults. One thing is sure, the man who cannot get up in the morning will catch few fish from the House Pool unless he is fortunate enough to find it vacant in the evening. Usually the swim is claimed at first light by an early riser and held grimly all day. Night fishing is strictly barred and a watch is kept for nocturnal prowlers by local Thames bailiffs.

Upstream the current runs over a gravelly shallow and narrows into a fast run before opening into a deep and slightly turbulent pool. There it shallows up again and continues downstream to a dense bed of lilies which covers almost the whole width of the stream. A fast fish can reach these lilies if firm pressure is not applied quickly, not withstanding the fact that they are some thirty yards away.

For some inexplicable reason the only really successful bait on this water is a piece of sausage or sausage meat. Fish there have been caught on cheese and bread pastes and I have taken a chub there on freshwater mussel, but as a rule it is the sausage which takes the greater toll of the fish.

In the close season of 1958 I contacted Mr Peter Stone of Wolvercote, the well-known Thames expert, with a view to learning more about the barbel in this water. Peter set to work with a plummet, studied the bottom and the current along the feeder and decided that the barbel ought to be in either of two places. He baited these places from time to time with half-cooked beef sausages and began to fish them in the open season. He was successful in that his first attempt produced a six pound fish and later another of eight pounds fell to a Mr Paul Goss who accompanied him on several occasions. During these experiments several roach approaching two pounds were taken on huge pieces of sausage, but were unable to give any account of themselves on the sturdy barbel tackle being used at the time.

I began to fish the House Pool whenever possible but apart from dace and an occasional chub I met with no success.

Weekends were bedlam for, as soon as it was heard that a few barbel were being caught, anglers were occupying space every few yards along the bank.

A couple of hours in the early morning was the most that one could hope for. (The water has always been heavily fished but as a rule the barbel are not expected until later in the year.)

I fished the House Pool on and off for a season without success and in 1959 I fished again through July and August without seeing a barbel. In September, however, following my success on the 'High Bank' and being brimful of confidence at having caught my first barbel, I went to the House Pool with a couple of pounds of sausages.

I had a feeling (one which I seldom get incidentally) that today would be my lucky day. I went *expecting* to catch a barbel, but I confess that I did not expect one quite so large as the one I caught!

Firstly I was undecided about tackle and put up an Avon type three-piece rod and a line of five pounds breaking strain. Then I decided to use a stronger line just in case I met up with a double figure fish. The only other line I had was one of nine pounds breaking strain, and realising that this would not be suitable for use with an Avon type rod, I dismantled it and put up a Mark IV. After that, of course, I thought I might as well use a complete carp outfit and tied on a No. 2 carp hook. A quarter-ounce lead, stopped a foot above the hook, completed the rig and I cast it out baited with half a large beef sausage.

It was about 6.30 am and I was joined then by a local night-worker who invariably fishes the House Pool before going home to bed. I spoke to him several times but he ignored me and I thought perhaps that he was annoyed to find his favourite swim occupied. I learned eventually, however, that he was unfortunately rather deaf and just hadn't heard me. I watched him miss several good bites while my bait remained untouched. I couldn't have said if the bites came from barbel or not but it occurred to me that he was casting into the shallow run above the pool. I decided to try my luck in the shallow run *below* it.

Within a minute my line began to slacken in a series of jerks and then suddenly began to tighten up. I struck and hooked something which decided that the lily bed downstream was a much nicer place than the one it was occupying at present, and set off in that direction at a frightening pace. I had to stop it and I was thankful that I had finally chosen the Mark IV outfit with which to fish. I think the fact that the fish was in shallow water made it move as fast as it did and as I clamped down on the reel I began to fear that even the carp tackle would not stop this fish.

I turned it, however, with less than a couple of feet to spare and it then made for the pool itself where it bored deep and strongly for a considerable time. I had a large landing net assembled, but it was out of my reach and while the fish was plunging madly below my rod I called three times to my companion. Then, realising that he could not hear me and was unaware of the situation, I let out an ear-piercing whistle which made him turn round. He sized up the situation, looked at his own net and decided it was too small. He picked up my large one and, while I was quite prepared to land my own fish, it seemed that he knew exactly what to do. I noticed that he slid the net into the water and kept still, waiting for me to bring the fish in. I have always hesitated to allow anyone I did not know to land my fish because I have seen too many excited net-wielders try to scoop fish out in a wild panic and cause a good fish to be lost. I need not have worried at all on this occasion because my companion only needed the one chance. After another brief fight the barbel slid over the rim of the net and was expertly lifted out on to the bank. I looked at it and thought that it might be double figures; my companion said it would weigh twelve pounds but a check on two independent balances confirmed its weight to be eleven and a quarter pounds. This was not an exceptional barbel by the record lists and fish much larger than this are caught each year from the Hampshire Avon. It is a good fish from any water, however, and a very good one from the Thames area.

Two days later a friend of mine, Mr Brian Cotteril, of Waddesdon, caught another fish of exactly the same weight from the House Pool, which he at first thought might be the same fish. Photographs of both fish were taken at the time of capture, however, and there is no doubt that they were different fish.

Larger fish have been caught from the House Pool and swims in this particular water but those mentioned are the only ones which I have been concerned with apart from smaller fish not worthy of mention. Even larger ones have been lost and fish of record breaking proportions have been seen there.

Whether they will be caught or not remains to be seen, but the fact that many double figure fish have been caught is largely due to the efforts of the local anglers, for it was they who discovered the 'secret of the sausages'.

# Weir-Pools, Worms, Tea and Barbel

*H. T. Sheringham*

What? Where? Yes, by Jove! I *do* see him. There he goes round that iron stay. The water's not more than 4 feet there, but he doesn't seem to mind the punt. Great red brute! I dare say he's 8 or 9 pounds. There he goes over the sill and back into the deep water. Take one of the worms? He might, but these big barbel are uncertain creatures. It isn't often that you get one 'promiscuous-like'.

Another perch? Good! have him in. No he shows silver - it's a roach. A 1/2 - pounder, and in quite good condition. No, it's quite true: roach don't take worms well in summer, except in ponds. But you are always likely to catch one or two in a weir-pool, especially early in the season. Perhaps the oxygen in a place like this makes them hungrier than they would be in the open stream. There's more oxygen in the weir-pool than elsewhere, because of the falling water, and that's why such a lot of fish come up into it after the spawning season. When you are run down you go to the seaside or to the mountains. It's just the same - what men of science call anthropomorphology. I only found out what that was the other day, which is why I'm telling you now.

Why don't they all stay in the weir-pool for ever? Because there's more food in other parts of the river - more weeds, and shrimps, and snails, and flies, and things like that. So they go back to find them.

*'The mountain sheep were sweeter,*
*But the valley sheep were fatter;*
*We therefore deemed it meter*
*To carry off the latter.'*

Do you know the history of Ionia? It is a tale of mountain race after mountain race migrating from the hungry uplands to the fat plains and staying there. The story of fishes in the Thames is just the same. Yes, of course some stay in the weir-pools. There are also people on mountains. But most Scotsmen are in London.

My fault? You had a terrific bite, and you tried to play him with the rod, and he's broken you? And it was the 9 pound barbel! My good sir, I didn't tell you to grasp the rod with both hands and hold on, with your eyes starting out of your head! If you'd let a little line start out of your reel it would have been more to the purpose. *Est modus in rebus*. It is the part of a proper angler to be ready for these emergencies.

Never mind; put on a new hook, and let me comfort you by calling your attention to that punt away down there. Yes, they are barbel-fishers. They've spent pounds and pounds in lobworms from Nottingham, and they've baited that swim for days. Why from Nottingham? Because that's where most of the lobworms come from. It's a regular industry, with master-wormers and sub-wormers. There was a strike last summer, and nobody could buy any lobworms in London at all. Yes, it seems quite right, as you are about to suggest, that a wormer should turn.

Oh no; you needn't buy them unless you want to. You go out on to the lawn after dark with a candle and a bucket, and you see the worms lying on the grass and grab them. It's very difficult, because they can slip into the ground again like a flash, but it's not bad fun. You are really expert when you can grab a worm with each hand and not break either. Yes, rather slimy, and it makes the back ache. Keep them in? Moss. It makes them tough and active. It puts them into training, but is apt to train them a bit too fine and then they die. I like a tub of moist earth with moss on top.

About the barbel-fishers? Oh yes, as I was saying, they've thrown in thousands of lobworms, and they started fishing at daybreak, and they've finished all their beer, and they haven't had a bite. How do I know? Well, I don't precisely know; I hazard what is called a shrewd guess. I've been barbel-fishing myself, you see. Oh, well, now and then, but never a really big day. You want to stick to it for that, and lobworms cost ten shillings a thousand. Besides, all our ideas about barbel are wrong, I'm sure.

Our method of barbel-fishing is to train the fish to take exotic foods, and then depend on the false taste which they have acquired. Worms are exotic to them when you throw them in in thousands in hot summer weather. Perhaps the barbel will acquire a taste for them, perhaps not. Then there is greaves. 'Are' greaves? Possibly; I don't know whether it is singular or plural, like the sub-editor who was heard to say to the sporting editor, "Here's two sticks about Keats. What *are* Keats?" And the sporting editor was not sure, but said he'd ask the vet.

You get greaves from the tallow-chandler, and I believe it is a residuum from tallow-chandling. I don't know any more about it, but I used to go and hunt for gentles in an old-fashioned chandler's establishment when I was a boy, and I can remember the smell to this day. They were beautiful gentles, nearly as big as wasp-grubs. I expect modern science has done away with that sort of thing, but I associate greaves with the old, old smell, and that's why I don't use it. Obviously it is not a food natural to barbel, and the experts say that if you throw in too much the fish soon get sick of it. I don't wonder!

What ought we to do? Obviously we ought to fish for barbel with the things that they eat normally. That's the trouble: we don't know what they eat, not really. And yet they must eat a great deal, because they grow so big, and they are very numerous, so we ought to be able to catch a great many. If I had a private barbel swim, I'd make all sorts of experiments. A mill-pool on the Kennet would be the ideal place, because the Kennet water is very clear, and you can often see right to the bottom. I believe water-snails, and fresh-water shrimps, and things like that, are the barbel's natural food. The trouble is putting them on a hook. Shrimps are tiny little things, and barbel hooks have to be pretty stout in the wire. Perhaps you could use some sticky stuff like seccotine, and simply stick four or five shrimps to the hook. Snails might be tied on with fine thread. Frenchmen use aniseed cake for many kinds of fish, and they tie it to their hooks with thread. They call it 'la noquette'. We don't know everything about fishing in England, though we think we do.

If we got elvers in the Thames nowadays, I believe they would be as good a bait for barbel as anything. It might be worth someone's while to get some from the Severn and try them. Chub take them ravenously in the Severn, but that river has no barbel. I should think elvers would travel well enough in damp weeds or moss very lightly packed. I seem to remember that they died when crowded in water in a bait-can.

Another perch? Well, you've made sure of your breakfast, anyhow. Have them cooked in their jackets. Cooks have a sort of idea that it is their business to remove the scales before cooking the fish. It's an absurd waste of time. We might just as well go and remove Wittenham Tump yonder with a spade before walking over it. Besides, perch are all the better for being cooked in their scales, and when they are cooked flesh and skin are very easily parted.

Two bites, and no result except half the worm gone each time! Perhaps they were from dace. Or perhaps the perch are just playing with the bait; they often do if they're not keen, and they've not been keen so far. Try the Pennell tackle. Not got any? Why, make it. Take two of these eyed hooks and tie them on to a strand of gut as shown in the figure below. Yes, 3 inches apart for these big lobworms. For small worms, don't have them quite so far apart, and use very small hooks. Put the worm on with one hook in the head and the other near the tail. Then, whether the fish takes the head or the tail, he'll find a hook in it. Perch generally take the head, but if they are just playing, they will sometimes tweak the tail. Dace generally go for the head and roach for the tail.

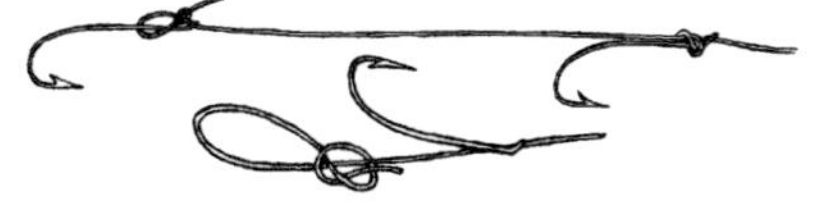

*Pennell Tackle*

Got him? A dace, as I thought. You can see *he's* in fine condition. Dace are the earliest spawners of all coarse fish, and they recover sooner in consequence. No, he's not worth putting in the well. He's only 7 inches long, so put him back. Ten inches is the measure of a large dace in the Thames, and you don't get too many of that size.

Yet another abortive bite. Probably it is a perch this time. I'll show you how to catch that fellow. Raise the point of the rod and pull the worm slowly up towards the surface. Now let it sink slowly. Now pull it slowly along in a slanting direction. There! do you feel a check? Let him have it. See the line travelling out into the stream of its own accord. Now strike gently. Got him! It's only a little thing, but that doesn't matter. You've learnt one of the most valuable secrets of perch-fishing, and that is the use of a moving bait. It is not always necessary, of course, but when the fish are not very keen, it is a sure way of catching one or two more.

Lunch-time? Yes, it is about. No, I've no particular theories about lunch, except that it ought to be a bigger affair in a punt than on the bank. You are doing less, therefore you must eat more. Yes, perfectly logical because it's English, like Sunday and four square meals between naps. Church? Of course, but the sermon tends to compose the mind and close the eyes. I'm not blaming anyone. Since you press me, I will say that marmalade sandwiches are one of the most valuable ingredients of a fishing lunch. They tend to reduce both hunger and thirst at the same time. An apple also. Sometimes my lunch consists of a piece of shortbread and a packet of chocolate. To tell the truth, I don't regard lunch as of very great importance. The sensation of hunger about one o'clock can be allayed by a very small meal. Tea is the important thing, and you should have it quite early, from 3.30 to 4 pm. Fishes have ceased to feed by about that time in summer, and begin again later. Yes, presently we will move over to the lock island and have some.

Too proud to have some of that pie? Far from it.

And I'll thank you for a lettuce also. Yes, a roll is more appetising than bread. No, it's all right; here are both salt and mustard, and the butter's in that little pot. Well, since you have got two bottles of lager beer, it would be a pity to waste them. There is another tin in the basket. Oh, cheese-cakes and tartlets! All excellent good. Lucullus will now lunch with himself.

★ ★ ★

Yes, it is sadly true; one does not feel so energetic after lunch. The sun also, as you observe, is hot. Very well, we'll drop down into the backwater and tie up under the shade.

*The Thames Style*

Why aren't we fixed across the stream like those other people? Well, personally, I don't know how to make a ryepeck stand upright in solid gravel - do you? I thought not. It's an art which I've never mastered.

Certainly, to be a complete Thames fisherman one ought to be able to do it, because otherwise one cannot fish in the Thames style. The Thames style doubtless has its advantages. It is less trouble to let the float travel downstream away from you and then to draw it back to the punt than to throw it in above you and then lift it out when it has got below you.

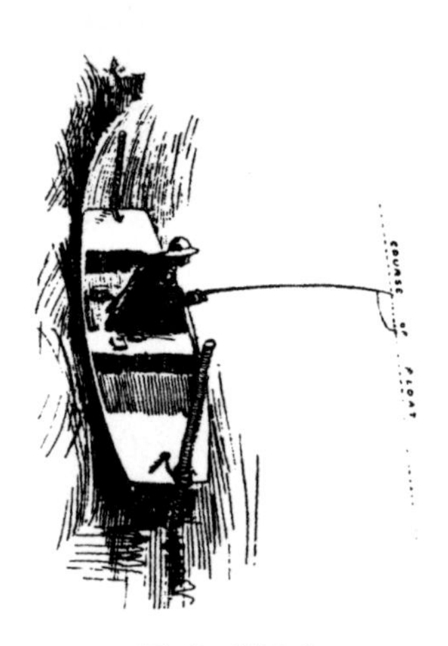


*The Parallel Style*

But it has disadvantages also, in my opinion, especially when you are fishing for rather shy biters like roach, which eject a bait on the least provocation. At the end of an ordinary Thames swim the hook is a long way from the point of the rod, and you have to strike rather forcibly; also, as you are striking upstream, there is a risk of pulling the hook out of the fish's mouth. When you are fishing in the other way, with the float travelling parallel with the punt, I think striking is more likely to be effective, as you are in much closer touch with your hook the whole time. Yes, towards the end of the swim you are also striking upstream, but not at nearly so acute an angle.

Bites? I didn't know you wanted bites as well as shade. You do? Well, then you'd better fish for gudgeon. You're not likely to catch much else here. It's too shallow for barbel, and rather clear for us to expect anything else. Put on a small hook - yes, that No. 11 will do - and bait with one of these brandlings. Fish just on the bottom. All right, but don't lose it. Some people have an idea that plummets are made to be lost. They are a convenience, but not a necessity. You can always make sure of the depth by shifting your float up or down. When you are too deep it drags. All you have to do is to reduce the depth a little until it just doesn't drag.

*The plummet and its use*

Not to put too fine a term upon it, brandlings come from manure-heaps. You find them sometimes in leaf-mould, but I think in that case there must have been a substratum of manure to encourage them. Unpleasant? Really, you provoke me to say that this is a finicking age. Full of humbug, too! People don't mind steeping their souls in all the garbage that passes for advanced literature or drama, but they shudder at the idea of picking a harmless brandling out of a ripe manure-heap. Is it not always possible to wash your hands when they seem to require it? But it isn't so easy to have a moral and intellectual bath. It seems to me that strong formalin solution . . . Yes, you're right - I digress.

To return to the brandlings. It's a queer thing, but you won't find them in all manure-heaps. Some are too young and moist, some too old and dry. You want your heap to be just ripe - that is to say, rich, binding well together, and reverting in pleasant fashion to Mother Earth. Sometimes you turn over quite a lot of it with the fork before you find any worms, and then just as despair grips you, behold there is a noble colony, lustrous and luscious. It is certainly one of the minor triumphs to come upon a store of brandlings after much fruitless digging. Picking them up as fast as your hand can fly from ground to tin is pleasurable. Human beings love picking things very fast, especially wild things - nuts, blackberries, mushrooms, and so on.

As a child one yearned for praise. I remember a lane where the violets used to grow in March, and where I used to pick like fury. Once I gained great credit for getting a whole bunch of white ones, which were rather rare in that district. But they always applauded me, which made me persevere instead of fishing for newts in the pond or small eels in the ditches. I have an idea now that I saved the grown-ups a good deal of stooping, and that therefore they said I was an able and diligent boy. But the kind sayings were welcome, and I am not sure that they would not be welcome now. If, for example, I was picking blackberries, I think I should be gratified at being applauded for zeal. With regard to brandlings, one has to be content, of course, with the applause of one's own conscience.

No, one does not grow out of all childish things, thank Heaven! You, I observe, now want to be praised for having caught eight gudgeon. Nine? It's pretty well considering, though people often catch ninety without being puffed up. But they rake for them. Raking is a species of ground-baiting. You have a huge iron rake on a long handle, and you stir up the gravel above the swim. This colours the water and, no doubt, dislodges all sorts of small creatures of which the fish are fond. These get carried down by the stream, and the gudgeon collect to feed on them. I don't know who first discovered this dodge, but he must have been an ingenious fellow. Presently we will angle for a big perch with one of those gudgeon.

Caught an odd fish? Let me look. Oh, that's what we used to call a 'daddy ruffe' in Gloucestershire. They call it a pope on the Thames, I think. So far as I know, it is of no use at all. It never grows big enough to eat. Perhaps it is designed as an encouragement to young anglers. It is a bold biter, and the veriest novice could hardly fail to catch it, if he fished in the right places. Like a little spotted perch? That describes it exactly.

Odd that the idea should have occurred to us both simultaneously. We will at once put across to the island and have some.

★ ★ ★

Yes, another cup, please. Milk in first. People *will* not realise that it makes all the difference to put the milk in first. It gives the tea quite a different and a much better taste. I am no chemist, but it is evident to me that the two processes of pouring hot tea into cold milk and cold milk into hot tea must give quite opposite results. Women nearly always say that they cannot measure the quantity of milk required till they see what colour the tea turns. That, I take it, betrays either laziness or incapacity to grasp essential truths. Really noble women, however, put the milk in first, without argumentative evasion. Men always do when they have thought about it.

No, I do not agree that it is a trifle unworthy of our consideration on a day's fishing. Few things concern the angler more than tea, and it is therefore of importance that he should have it at its best. Whisky? He that will to Cupar of course maun to Cupar, and no doubt whisky is all very well for those who benefit by it. Personally, I only value it as a febrifuge after getting very wet. For a mild stimulant on a long day's fishing give me tea. It refreshes not only the body, but the brain, and you need an active brain for fishing. Whisky, so far as I have been able to observe, stimulates the body at the expense of the brain. But the two together have their use when you are very exhausted or have been out all day in heavy rain. Do you know Barry Pain's imitation of Burns in 'The Poets at Tea':

*'Weel, gin ye speir, I'm no inclined,*
*Whusky or tay, to state my mind*
*For ane or ither;*
*For, gin I tak the first, I'm fou,*
*And, gin the next, I'm dull as you.*
*Mix a' thegither.'*

There is perhaps some value in compromise here as elsewhere.

*Suave mari magno* . . . Is there anything pleasanter in life than to sit, refreshed with tea, on a shady lock island, and to watch one's fellow-creatures struggling along on the bosom of Father Thames? Nowhere can people acquire such a look of heated exhaustion as on the river. See those two determined men, whose object is to get certainly to Abingdon, possibly to Oxford, ere nightfall. They take their pleasures arduously, that kind. Not that I deny a pleasure in your steady ten-mile pull. Exercise in itself is a joy, with the straining of muscles and the consciousness of strength applied. Then there is the delight of rhythm, four sculls moving in exact unison, and the skiff leaping responsive to every stroke. And the lip-lap of the water, the jewelled drops falling from the feathered blades, the masterful shout of "Lo-ock!" - all these and other things are to be reckoned up. But chiefly there is the eating up of miles. Men love to eat up miles.

Equally there is no place where people can look so cool and comfortable as on the Thames. Look at that Canadian canoe and its freight! They have come, perhaps, from Shillingford since lunch - about two miles in three hours, so there is no reason why they should look overworked. But they are ready for their tea, as all decent people should be. Without wishing to institute comparisons, I am quite sure that tea poured out by those pretty hands would be superlative. I have a weakness for that particular combination of dark eyelashes and grey-blue eyes. The hair too . . . Yes, yes, let us be going. Still, I'm sure she'd pour the milk in first, and he's a lucky fellow. Sentimental? Well, well! *Et ego in Arcadia vixi*. The river serves other purposes besides those of the angler, and who are we to question? I seem to remember that you also . . . but no matter.

Ah! the barbel still rankles? Have at another, then. We'll try the run between the rushes and the corner of the island. It's deep, gravelly, and streamy, the combination best suited for barbel. We'll fasten at the corner of the rushes and cast our legers down into the deep hole. Frankly, I have not much hope of catching one, but the swim is baited sometimes, so it is just worth trying.

This is the tackle I prefer. The traditional Thames leger-lead is a flat thing threaded on to a strand of gimp, which is fastened in the middle of the gut-trace. I don't like the combination of gut and gimp, somehow, and I would sooner have my lead on the reel-line. This is what is called a paternoster lead, but it does very well for legering. The line runs through the ring very freely, which is an advantage. A No. 6 hook and a lobworm hooked by the middle and you're ready. Pull a dozen yards off your reel and coil it on the bottom of the punt as you pull it off. Now lay your rod across the punt and reverse the coils, so that the bottom one consists of the line nearest the reel, and the top one of the line nearest the first ring on the rod. Now pick up the rod and swing the lead back, holding the line meanwhile in your left hand. Now swing the lead forward, let the line go, and you will see the bait travel away to the desired spot. As it goes, the line is picked up from the bottom of the punt coil by coil, until a click from the reel shows that it is all out. Let the lead reach the bottom and then tighten till you can just feel it. When, and if, a bite comes, you will feel that too.

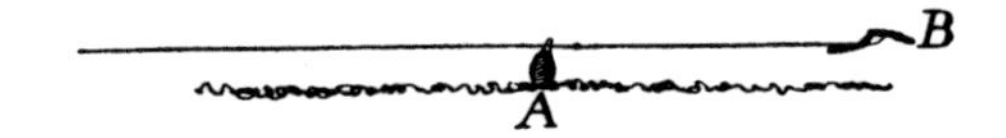


*Leger-tackle (a to b = 24 to 36 inches).*

This ability to cast a bait out from the coil is a necessary accomplishment, but it is very easily learnt. With a small amount of practice you will be able to throw a ½-ounce lead 30 yards, which is as much as is generally necessary. A heavy pike-bait can, in favourable circumstances, be thrown 60 yards, but you cannot make much of a job of fishing at so great a distance. The other way of casting is from the reel, as to which it is too late in the day to say anything now. Perhaps another time. It is rather a depressing subject. I acquired what small skill in it I possess in that meadow yonder, and woundily I smote myself with leads, horribly I involved myself in tangles, gravely I imperilled my future by bad language, during several hours of two days. At length I emerged victorious.

But my friend Polylogus picked up the knack of it in half an hour, and is of the opinion that there is nothing much in it. True, I was at his elbow, while at my elbow there was no one, but even so it appears to me that things are not evenly distributed. Polylogus hardly had to swear at all, and it does not seem right.

Yes, it's a slow game, this legering, when bites do not come. It is one of the poorest forms of fishing to my mind, because you're doing nothing and there's nothing to look at. When you've got a float to watch, there always seems to be a prospect of something happening immediately. And floats often bob in a hopeful way for no particular reason, or rather for no reason connected with the hook. Very young fishes have a playful habit of butting at your float or rubbing themselves against it, and that sort of thing makes it bob. Often, moreover, I believe that older fish push against the gut cast as they cruise about at the bottom, and that, again, makes the float bob. Once or twice I have seen a pike or perch assault a fat cork float, which is a cheery spectacle. Then, again, a dragon-fly or a wasp will settle on it, and that is interesting. A float is a great dispeller of ennui.

Yes, that is what one *does* want, to have the curtain

of water withdrawn for a brief space, and to see what fish lurk in those mysterious depths. If I have heard one man utter such a wish, I have heard a hundred. But I have never known their prayer answered in any way. The river always preserves its undisturbed reticence. Nay, not always. A day comes now and then when the water is very clear and the light at the proper angle, and then you may see a good deal, enough to fascinate you with the underwater world. It is a world of hill and valley, plain and grove, just like ours, and, on the whole, its inhabitants are not unlike us. They are perhaps a little more candid in their manner of devouring each other. They do not, so far as I know, talk about the laws of supply and demand, or promulgate doctrines about the survival of the fittest. Not that I blame us – far from it. If I am to be devoured, I would much rather have it done tactfully by a minister with golden words in his rotund mouth. Socialists remind me of pike, which have no tact.

Hullo! you appear to have hooked something. A slow, dragging sort of bite? I don't know what it may be. A barbel generally gives two sharp tugs. Whatever it is, it is fighting well. Don't hurry it. There's lots of time. Yes, you were quite right to let the line off the reel then. You see, you are a long way from your fish, and it is in strongish water. Now then, reel it up. It's coming. I believe it *is* a barbel after all; I saw a gleam of reddish copper. Now I can see it, and it's only a small one - foul-hooked, I believe. Yes, there you are. See, it's hooked in the ventral fin. A 3-pounder or thereabouts. It illustrates what I was saying just now, about fish rubbing against the line, and it explains that dragging bite. The fish was rooting on the bottom, and got foul of the hook. Barbel often do that, and if you hook a big one on roach tackle in this way you think that the fight is going to last for ever. They are very strong fish, and when hooked foul are doubly strong, of course. All right, we'll put him in the well for the time being.

Trout? Well, the chance of a Thames trout in these days is not worth much to the casual fisherman. If you are on the river every day you may catch a few, but it's an uncertain game. Most of the big ones are well known, and are fished for by determined fellows who grudge no amount of time and trouble to the pursuit. I have hooked three Thames trout in my time, landing one of them. And I once rose two beauties in this very pool with a salmon-fly. The trout I landed was between 7 and 8 inches long, and till I have very convincing proof to the contrary, I shall consider myself entitled to the fame of having caught the smallest Thames trout on record. I am not, I hope, a vain man, but I cling to my rights.

He was a funny little fish, and he lived in a funny little hole between two stones in the extreme right-hand corner of Benson weir-pool, where a small over-flow of water from the main fall made a special little stream for him. I was fishing for perch with a worm, and had caught two or three in or close to this hole, when the little trout got hooked. I unhooked him, carried him to the quiet water of the open pool about 20 yards away, and placed him gently in. With a pleased wag of the tail he departed. Then I returned to my perch-fishing. Nothing happened to disturb my meditations for some time, and about a quarter of an hour later I was looking idly at the water, when I saw a small figure making its way up the rough water close to my feet. It was my small trout! He swam slowly but purposefully back to his little hole, and there, for all I know, he abides to this day.

Yes, you are right; I *do* feel an affection for that little fish, and, indeed, for all little fish. They are cheery, companionable creatures, and I cannot explain the instinct which makes me want to catch them. It certainly seems illogical, and the humanitarians can make out a case which is specious on the face of it. But when you come to think seriously, you see that they are only playing on the surface of things. Sport is an intrinsic part of the world-scheme. The spider quite obviously takes an interest in his pursuit of a fly; the dog finds most of his life-pleasure in hunting rabbits; and even the rabbit feels a thrill at sight of a defenceless lettuce.

It is no good telling me that a lettuce does not feel. The principle of life is in a lettuce just as much as in you or me. And your humanitarian will eat lettuces without a pang, also nuts, and apples, and perhaps even eggs. On his own showing he is therefore a brutal fellow, since he is interfering with the principle of life, diverting it from its natural development. Were he to be consistent, he would eat nothing, drink nothing, and cease to breathe, for whatever he does he interferes. So he would die. And even in dying he would be in the wrong of it, since wilfully, of malice prepense, he would have interfered with the development of the life principle within himself. And that is obviously a wrong thing to do.

No; your rabid humanitarian who wants us to give up sport is in a cleft stick. There is no logical way for him to tread. Why, there is brave sport going on within him every day and every hour of the day, even a kind of fishing! In the warm stream of his blood are great battles, leucocytes preying upon bacilli, bacilli marshalling their array against leucocytes. And he is powerless to prevent it. Even if he dies, what happens? His atoms continue the unending conflict, and the very worms that were himself turn one against another. I am profoundly sorry for the man who sees evil, and nothing but evil, in 'Nature red in tooth and claw'. There is nothing before him but the abyss of despair, for how can he endure to go on living in a scheme which makes him an unwilling instrument of red ruin and death so long as his entities exist, and that is so long as this physical world lasts?

This is no philosophy for us anglers, conscious as we are by frequent intercourse with Nature of a scheme which is intrinsically good and not evil. Look at that wagtail on the end of the beam there. It is a terrible instrument of destruction, that dainty, humorous, happy little thing. The amount of life which that monster destroys every day would make you shudder could you realise it in the true pessimistic spirit. But see if you can detect any signs of remorse in those bright eyes or that perky tail. No, of course you can't, because it is right that the bird should do these distressing things, just as it is *right* that you, living in this part of the world, should from time to time eat beef - beef being the result of the regrettable decease of ox. The truth, as I see it, is that the life-principle in all created things is lent, not given, and it must in due course be returned to the hand that lent it. The manner of that return is not for creatures to choose, nor does it matter.

We all - men, beasts, birds, fishes, plants - have it in common. How does it concern us in what way it passes from one to another, or which of us for the moment gives it outward form? Thinkers are too much obsessed with the idea of individualism, which is really quite another matter. If by a simple process you become an intrinsic portion of a crocodile, naturally you cease to be the handsome fellow who aforetime sat in this punt and wondered why he did not get any more bites. But you don't stop: you go on.

You think that I had better stop? Yes, you are right, and, in fact, I'm getting rather perplexed myself. The problem of the soul wants rather more attention than I have been able to give it so far. A million years hence, if we can then conveniently discuss things ... But there is one more thing with regard to this humanitarianism. It is evidently meant that we should be responsible for the divergence of the vital principle - that is to say, for death in one form or another. But I grant importance in our mental attitude. There must be no malice. We must not desire to kill simply for the sake of killing, because that reacts on our own natures, besides causing more death than Nature requires. It would be evil to drain a pond dry simply that its inhabitants might gasp away their lives for man's edification, and afterwards lie there to rot. But it is not evil to try and catch them with a hook or (otherwise than in sporting sense) with a net. Our interest lies not in the killing, but in the contest of wits and skill, in the eating, or perhaps in profit to be made. We are developing natural and healthy faculties, not pandering to a morbid lust of cruelty. It is possible, I maintain for a sportsman to feel for his quarry both respect and affection, and yet to pursue it none the less. Does this seem a hard saying? Yet you may prove it by the fatherly eye which a fishery owner casts on his fish, and the arrangements he makes for their health and comfort. Nothing is more saddening to an honest angler than the sight of fish dying in polluted water, and that is chiefly because he looks on fish as his familiar friends, and grieves that they should be so sadly used.

You begin to find your friendly feelings wearing thin? Well, let us try and catch something more. This barbel hole is unremunerative, but I see signs of activity by the camp-sheathing there. Look at that little wave rippling along the beam. That's a perch for certain, hard at work getting his supper. There's another. At this time of the evening you may often see perch close in to the sides of locks and weirs and walls. We'll move the punt round to the other side of the point, and try to catch one or two of those fellows from the shore. Put on my float tackle while I paddle round; yours has only got the tiny hook on it.

Let's have the smallest of those gudgeon you caught out of the well. Here's the little hand-net. Now put him on your hook by the corner of the lip. Get out of the punt and drop the bait in close to the camp-sheathing, just where we saw the perch feed. Let it sink slowly, and then keep the float in the same place. There, it's off! Let him have it a bit. Now tighten. Not got him? The gudgeon's all right, so the perch can't have meant business. Try again. The same result? Evidently the gudgeon's not what they want.

We'll try a small worm on that gudgeon hook. When perch are not very keen sometimes that will tempt them. Now then, sink and draw it quite close to the piles, just as you did when you got that fish before lunch. Not too deep; the fish are evidently not far from the top. There you are - got him at once. Easy with him; that roach hook is on very fine gut. I'll get the landing-net. Here he is; not far off $^3/_4$ pound. Go and catch another.

When you find perch on the feed it's as well to waste no time, especially when there isn't much daylight left. I don't think they are so prone to bite in the evening as some other fish, and you never know how long they'll go on. Hullo! that's not a perch this time, unless it's a monster. That steady run might almost be a trout.

Yes, let him have line if he wants it. He's a biggish fish. Handle him lightly, or you'll never see him at all with that gut. Now you've turned him. Get your line back steadily and keep your rod-point up. No, I haven't seen a sign of him yet; he's playing deep. I think I saw a gleam then. Yes, it's a big chub. Now you can see him yourself. He's nearly ready for the net. Let the stream carry him down into it. There you are; and a very nice fish, $3^1/_2$ pounds if he's an ounce. It does you credit to have landed him on a fine roach-hook.

Yes, it's time we were off, if we are to have any supper. You don't want to keep the barbel, do you? Here he goes back into the river, then. We'll give the chub to one of the villagers, and have the perch for breakfast. The gudgeon will be all right in the well. Now for home.

You feel as if you'd like to sing? Yes, I understand. If you were a quartette, I would beg you to do so. A quartette on the water at dusk is a delicious thing. You want soft harmonies to blend with the slumber-song of the river. A duet? I think, perhaps, it would be better if I resumed the topic which you cut short a while ago. The pale fires of night begin to inspire me with a hope that, after all, we can attain to some comprehension of what, under the sun, seemed incomprehensible. After all, the soul . . .

# A Midnight Battle with a Monster Barbel

*J. L. Webb*

Tench, carp, and barbel fishing are akin; all three need the patience of Job, warm, still weather, and early morning or late at night are the best times to try conclusions with the patriarchs.

It is only at those times that the great barbel get on the move; during the day they seem to seek the solitary weed-beds or deep weir pools, perhaps they never move at all during the daylight hours. We may picture them, bearded and shark-like; all through the burning hours they lie aloof and still among the sombre depths. Punts and boats pass overhead, pretty girls perhaps, reclining upon cushions, poled by sleek and adoring young men; noisy boating parties with their shrieking, giggling crews; patient fishermen sitting upon their camp stools and large wicker baskets, moodily regarding motionless floats or monotonously tweaking out infant perch and roach; the red and white cattle dreaming under the willows; the splashing and larking people bathing in the shallows; all these things do not affect those wise grandfathers of the finny tribe, perhaps they sleep (if fish can do such a thing, though it is hard to imagine any form of sleep coming to those lidless jewelled eyes) perhaps they dream . . . who knows?

But when at last the picnic parties depart and the bathing belles and fishermen also pack up and take their leave, when the sun leaves the water and the cattle go plodding away to distant farmyards in the water meadows, then the giants awake, refreshed!

There are some Thames fishermen who believe that a twenty-pound barbel is not an impossibility. Some of these men are professionals, they have 'had some', meaning that they have been broken by gigantic fish at that time the bats come out, and even the courting couples have left the river to darkness and to barbel fishers.

Here then is a true story of a battle with a giant barbel, and it comes from the Thames. The fisherman's name is Mr J. L. Webb of Reading, one of those who believe that a 20 lb barbel is no figure of the imagination, and this is his story:

I have taken many barbel, both from the Kennet at Reading, at Burghfield, and at various posts on the river Thames. I am a professional fisherman and my boats are moored at Moulsford Grange, Berkshire. For barbel fishing I use number eight hooks and five or six x drawn gut. Barbel are the fish I simply live for, it means a lot to me to be a barbel fisher, sir, one has to go without many things, including sleep, and you must possess great patience, both in waiting for the fish to take hold and in baiting up.

*(I break in here to observe that Mr Webb must be an angler after my own heart, I like his way of putting it - 'it means a lot to me to be a barbel fisher'.) He goes on to say:*

When roach fishers are catching roach the barbel fisher never gets a full basket. Well, it was an evening in September 1943. For some days previous I had been fishing a spot opposite the third meadow below the French Horn Hotel at Sonning, and had been baiting this spot for some time, though I had caught nothing but fish up to 7 lb, and few at that.

Well, this particular evening I had caught nothing and had had no bites; not even an eel, roach, or perch, came to break the monotony. In fact my father had said to me before I came out that it wasn't worth going as it wasn't the right sort of evening. But I told him that I was going to catch a big barbel there. You see, I have been a barbel fisher for forty years.

So I began to fish. I was using a fourteen-footer bank rod with a split cane top, an Allcock's reel with 150 yards of undressed silk line on it. I had gone over it carefully to see there was no faulty place and it seemed all right.

Somehow I thought I was going to get a two-figure fish that evening, I don't know quite why; on the other hand I might be going to have a blank. It was a dead flat calm. I had plenty of lobs and a nice place to sit and wait. I baited up my eight-hook with a big lob through the head and threw it out, well out, into the river. For the next hour nothing happened save once a small perch pulled at the bait. I had ground-baited with chopped worms, but nothing moved save a chub or two under some bushes and a few roach. Now the light was going fast and night was all but come. An owl got up out of a nearby wood and passed by me. I rebaited once more and cast out again. A friend came along and I had a cigarette from him which I lit. A few plover passed overhead, otherwise there was nothing to break the solitude. I couldn't see no farther than the end of my rod. A moorhen was moving about not far away and some rats splashed in some rushes.

Suddenly I feels a steady pull on the line and holding firmly for half a minute (for that is as long as you will 'hold' with a barbel) I struck, and felt a fast movement down-river which sent me to my feet. It was surely a pretty big fish. The line was running freely through the rings. There are some who say that a barbel does not move much, but that first mad rush was more like a devil from hell. After his first plunge he seemed to go broadside on to me, then his nose went down and he seemed to be trying to hit the line with his tail. What a time that was! I brought pressure to bear on him and that is more or less the supreme moment in barbel fishing, unless it is when he is coming to the net. The pressure I put on him was steady, but the fish was now at least fifty yards from me and still heading down-river. Then he changed his tactics. Down-stream from me was a fair-sized hedge and at all costs he must not go down there or he would get me smashed up in the roots which go into the river at that spot. You must remember by now it was nearly dark and my watch showed it was ten minutes to nine which meant I had had him on for twenty minutes and he was still heading downstream as fast as he could go. More pressure was urgent. I must turn him, so I applied more pressure. I prayed the gut would hold. Well, at that the fish slowed and little by little I brought him back, though he was trying to turn all the time. Then he turned again and headed downstream as hard as he could go and I thought the line must break. Still he hadn't showed himself. Then I coaxed him back again. How my heart beat! Getting tired he was, no doubt of that, so the fight went on. At long last he strikes surface and showed me his snout. At that off he went again downstream, but he was tiring. After a time I began to look around me for a landing-place. I mean a place where I could bring him in. God was good to me that night, for just then the moon peeped out and I saw two concrete slabs a foot or so from the bank. I unhooked my landing net. The time was just one hour and twenty minutes since he first broke surface. But he was not yet mine for he was still trying to get away downstream. But the pressure I brought to bear was burning him up and he surfaced this time close by and just quietly swam away. I got him in again coming broadside, I sees his mighty tail give a flap and he was swimming in again to me as I stood on those concrete slabs. I could see his yellowy white belly there in the half dark. Then he made a last bid for freedom. It was no use, his strength was near spent, and next time he comes in, I thought, you will be mine, either that or the battle would be lost. But God was good that night to me. I steadily bore him towards the net, waiting for the right moment. Then I had the net ring under him, twelve pound he was. He was mine at last. He was not my largest barbel, but that is another story!

So ended (this time successfully) that grim fight in the dark. I cannot help speculating on what that fish would have weighed had he got away in those last crucial moments. Not that I am casting doubt on the veracity of fishermen in general, but the fish that get away add pounds to their true weight.

But Mr Webb deserved this magnificent fish and I am only too happy to set his battle down on record. It was no mean feat to land it in the dark on fine tackle. I can so well picture the scene by the quiet river that September night, the dark trees and gleaming water, and that giant fish fighting for every inch of its life. Such happenings never depart from memory. It may be Mr Webb will never have another barbel of such a size, yet he will live in hopes, that I will warrant, and many another summer's evening will find him in the vicinity of 'the third meadow below the French Horn at Sonning' wooing a fish of even greater weight and calibre than this twelve-pound prize which gave him such a memorable time. When the fish was landed Mr Webb says the time was twenty minutes to midnight. The fight had lasted over three hours. I can imagine he slept well.

It may conceivably be that fishermen are less truthful than other men, I do not know. But I do know that fishermen do not mind - when they are talking with one another - *exaggerating* the size of fish, or the pain and disappointment of battles. Indeed I suspect that stories of great fish caught and lost (mostly lost) are looked for, nay, demanded, by the fisherman's inner self, they act as a tonic and gird him to greater endeavour. The trouble is that sometimes the angler *does* hook and lose a specimen fish, a record fish; by its very size and power it breaks free and departs. When we come to think of it, it is a wonder that any of the record fish have been landed. Indeed I doubt whether the record fish has ever been landed! The biggest on record have been netted or have been found gasping out their lives on the mud of drained ponds. And an angler is quite ready to believe the stories of his fellows, he rarely doubts them, unlike the layman who scoffs and makes fun of us. Those miserable mortals would not have the patience, let alone the skill, to catch a big fish, so we will not waste words upon them.

And so not all the accounts in this book are of great fish caught, some are of great fish hooked and lost, mostly at the last moment just when success seemed certain. No one can know the agony of such a catastrophe, no non-angler, that is, they cannot know the dreadful disappointment which lasts so long afterwards and recurs at intervals perhaps throughout life. The vast majority of fishermen have had such moments which they cannot recall without a pang, they feel again the old agony.

It is a fact that after a tussle with a big fish one always finds oneself 'all of a tremble', the hands quiver, the heart beats fast. Mentally and physically one feels 'whacked'. It is not the physical exertion but the intense excitement, the brain has been keyed up over a long period and many feel as though they have run a great race.

This fact will have been noticed in the accounts by fishermen in this book. The layman may seize upon this fact with a howl of derisive mirth, but let him laugh ... as the crackling of thorns under a pot, etc ...

Mr Webb's account of catching the big barbel is only one of several I have had from him. I doubt whether there is any other man in these islands who knows more about this particular species. He is essentially, first and foremost, a 'barbel man' just as there are carp men, bream men, pike and trout men. One fellow I know will fish for nothing but perch.

But one of Mr Webb's accounts must go into this book. I have had to do little editing of his letter and have tried to preserve his own, may I say, quaint way of putting things. I have already mentioned that Mr Webb believes that this species tops twenty pounds, though there is no authentic record (so far) of a fish of that weight being either netted or captured. The record to date is an account of one of sixteen pounds ten ounces caught on a night line from the Trent below Carlton Mill.

It must be sheer bad luck that Mr Webb does not head the list, for he once had what he swears was a twenty-pound barbel almost grassed. This is his account, slightly condensed:

I have made a special study of barbel, both in the Thames and the river Kennet. I know their feeding times, river conditions and all their favourite haunts. I now give you an account of a barbel which I honestly believe was upwards of twenty pounds.

The time was July 1926. I decided to fish a spot below the weir mills at Southcote. I had been very ill and as soon as I got home again I found the call of the river Thames and Kennet was strong in me and I had no time for greeting old friends so I prepared for an early morning's overture at the riverside. I decided to go to the Kennet because there was more flow and the weather was warm. I made up my tackle overnight, ground-bait I left to the morning, and so to bed I went, sir, but could not sleep. So downstairs I came, dressed, and read a book on fly tying. At 4 am having had a cup of tea, or 'you and me' as I calls it, I started out alone across the park. The morning was clear, there was not much mist, but the grass underfoot was wet.

There was a mist over the river. I passed the site of a haunted house and over the Holy Brook and there I could hear the barbel a-sucking in the weeds. Cattle rose from their slumbers in the water meadows and herons flapped overhead. I approached the tail of the mill stream. Daylight was now approaching. I cast out a few balls of bread made up solid into the swim. I fitted up with fifty yards of undressed line on a Nottingham centre-pin reel, thirteen-foot whole cane with a whalebone tip. I threaded 1/2-oz coffin lead on the gut which was checked by a small lead some eighteen inches from the hook, a number eight Sowerbutts. I baited up with bread paste the size of a walnut and cast it out into the swim. Then I settled down to wait. There was no breeze at all. It was so quiet that a heron came and stood in the reeds opposite to me, then it saw me and flew off with a great flapping of wings. Soon I had hooked a chub of four pounds, and later, landed a barbel of seven pounds. This was encouraging, it showed the fish were there.

I fished on until nine o'clock and then went home

to breakfast for I had made up my mind to come again in the evening. After having had my breakfast I took the barbel I had caught and sold it to a Mrs Millet of Millet's Stores, who used to live in Oxford Road, Reading. I regret she has now passed on to a more contented life. She was of the Jewish faith.

That evening I went back to the river with my father. Poor Dad had not enough patience for barbel fishing, pike were more in his line. Barbel over seven pounds become very crafty and you have to sit for days before you catch one.

It was a hot and sultry evening and as it was still too early for fishing I claimed my place and sat down under a willow to make a landing net as mine was getting the worse for wear. After a while the sun began to sink; other anglers were beginning to pass along the tow-path and some said "good-night". Bathers and other people were now also leaving the river and after a while my father comes along with a few small perch and jack he had caught. I reminded him I was quite happy to be left alone, but he stayed on.

Soon it was twilight with some cloud in the west. I could not have had a better night for barbel. Father began to grumble and just then the rod point was pulled right down and the line screamed off the reel. "That's done it," I said to Dad, "I shall be late now."

The fish was off downstream. "What is it?" asked Dad. "Barbel," I said, "without a doubt." "Hold him," said Dad. Poor Father, I just looked at him, how little he knew the ways of barbel! The fish was still boring down-stream and my father was still pleading for me to hurry. "Can't you turn him?" he said again, and he kept on like that until I had to speak sharply. "For goodness' sake, hold your peace!"

My mind was now occupied with the barbel which was now giving me a nose-down, broadside plunge, under the other bank. The line was out to the backing and still I could not check him. Then he went down and sulked until my father said he was round something for I couldn't move him; he was as stubborn as a rock. Then he began to move upstream again.

*(I here miss out some of Mr Webb's account as it is simply a description of the great fish fighting back and forth with rushes and borings, now under his bank, now opposite, and of his father getting more and more impatient all the time. At last the fish began to tire, after making as if it was going up the mill stream.) He goes on:*

The fish was now close under the rod point. Dad had ceased his mutterings, for the great moment was at hand. The fish was in nine or ten feet of water and after one more plunge began to come towards the surface. It had lain on its side as if it was beaten and I knew by the feel he was coming in nose first.

Father gets hold of the landing net and at that moment the fish breaks water in a great swirl of water, showing his complete body and tail just as my father turned the torch on him. Now he was a yard from my feet and what a fish. My God, I thought, *what* a fish!

*But again that great barbel got away from Mr Webb and still that grim battle went on by the dark river. At last it came in once more:*

It looked as though he was ours. My father now stood by with the landing net; I could hear his heavy breathing as he tried to get it under it, but the net was too small and just as that moment the gut, after so much strain, parted and that giant barbel was gone for good.

And so, says Mr Webb simply, 'we went home to bed.' We shall never know how much that fish weighed, but I know how bad Mr Webb must have felt as he and his father took their way homewards across the warm summer fields where the sleeping cows lay among the river mists. I see no reason why that barbel should not have weighed every ounce of twenty pounds. Mr Webb must have an expert eye. The battle had lasted for *two hours.*

## The Upper Thames

*John Ginifer*

It is one of life's little ironies that I have been asked to write this chapter about the upper Thames, for in many ways I am better qualified to write descriptively of those early rivers of my barbel interests. The Stour, so often temptingly clear, yet seldom easy, the Avon, fast and furious in current and often so in sport, and more especially the Kennet, the personal source of so many delightful barbelling days. Yet before you skip the rest, let me explain that whilst my experience of the Thames rests upon but five exciting years, little did I realise when introduced to it how shortly would the sum of all my previous fish be crowned with a series of ten- and eleven-pound barbel.

Thames fishing coincided with a subtle, yet radical change of attitude on my part to upstream legering. For years I had used this method on and off, more as a standby to offset swim peculiarities than as a primary method in its own right. Almost inevitably my first Thames barbel was caught conventionally downstream legering, in the middle of a memorable autumn morning - an initial chance that fortunately was not to blind me to the prime difficulty of hooking these fine, fat fish - the hurdle of bite detection!

Along a series of streamy shallow runs, alternated by deeper, yet quite fast swims, dace bites could be almost guaranteed in the middle of the day, given the introduction of a little groundbait. Yet, move a yard or so up or down in certain swims, and the dace bites vanished, the odd 'nibble' resulting in virtually no further signs of interest. The closer the approach of evening the more apparent this phenomenon of bites or no bites.

Without labouring the point, the discerning reader will realise that the evidence of biteless zones induced me to speculate that the presence of barbel was the most likely cause. Downstream legering tactics, done as sensitively as I knew how, failed to confirm the accuracy of my observations and led to a change of method - up and across stream legering.

Little by little success was forthcoming. A picture emerged that, if not clear-cut, held at least enough consistency to serve as a yard-stick for further development. During the day, the barbel appeared either to feed spasmodically or move along the swims, giving the appearance of irregular feeding. Later details will show how we used this knowledge to good effect, according to the conditions. As evening approached, however, we concentrated upon 'hot-spots' which called for accurate location and casting. Unless conditions were exceptional there was a definite limit to the number of chances one could expect each evening in a swim. How vividly I remember the mounting anticipation as light thickens, the sickening compulsion to inch the tackle downstream to confirm that all is well, that nerve-startling lift and drop of line as a big barbel 'takes'. Then the furiously fast swing of rod to make contact with that cause of downstream line curvature, and the rod-plunging, reel-grinding thrill that pays for all. Or that bemused, standing-to-attention, rod-in-air, curse-accompanied attitude that reveals a clean miss and foolish incompetence, inevitably and deservedly summarised by companions' comments.

So much for generalities of approach. Let us move to those details that in their sum make for the vital difference between fish or no fish. Location of suitable swims is so obvious an essential that one is loath to state the obvious, but in a river generally too coloured to allow for direct observation, it is easy to underplay this aspect. Miles and miles of mainstream and backwater barbel swims cry out for detailed attention. Some are regularly attended, but relatively few are actually fished in a manner specifically suited to reveal barbel potential.

Do not direct all attention to fast swims, but rather look for clean and hard bottoms, particularly in those steady swims near faster shallows. I try to fish as close to the barbel as possible, for as later comments will reveal, I place an emphasis on sensitive bite detection above all else. Repeatedly does one hear that Thames barbel are used to bankside visitors. Agreed - but so too are they used to fishermen, and act accordingly. As I am advising a close approach to these fish, I stress quietness, and slow movement - the clearer the conditions, the greater the need for acute control of bankside activity.

If you cannot bring yourself to reduce the odds against by a close study of a water, its depths, the nature of its bed, and so forth, then your chances will be reduced considerably. In waters that I have fished for years, I still spend as much time studying them, as actually fishing them - really it is one and the same thing, if you think about it.

So much for 'where'. Although the actual manner of fishing is now our concern, the emphasis is still upon a sensitive approach. I find that a rod of 12 ft has distinct advantages over shorter ones of say 10 ft or so. To be suited to my needs it must have a sensitive tip and be flexible enough in its middle and lower joints to allow powerful pressure to be applied. I use the 12 ft 'Hunter', all split cane, hollow-built in bottom joint, Chapman rod, and consider it the best one at present on the market, to suit my needs. It is light, yet when handled properly, has proved itself strong enough to bring several 10- and 11-pounders to net.

"Why twelve feet long?" you pointedly inquire, and I must adequately answer. Basically, I strive to use as light a lead as possible, setting the line in such a way as to reduce the current drag upon the tackle to the minimum and allow an early detection of bites by virtue of line movement. Of course, it is impossible to avoid all drag, but the difference between a line cast downstream, and pulled tight by the current, and one set differently is a critical difference. In the above circumstances the fish feels the initial weight of the tackle, which increases as the bait is moved downstream. Cautious 10-pounders are reluctant to pick up such a bait and set off downstream regardless of increasing pressure. They approach and suck it cautiously, then generally give it a wide berth - at best the angler is conscious of a 'nibble'. I recommend that you cast upstream, or across and upstream, with a leger super-sensitively set. By holding up the longer rod, as much line as possible is kept out of the fast current, thus reducing the drag. It is also easier to avoid the action of powerful eddies or other disadvantages of peculiar current set. When upstream legering I endeavour to strike at the 'sharp shiver' that generally precedes the line falling back downstream - frequently, I have hooked a downstream moving fish on the second or third strike, which at least points to the fact that the fish had not ejected the bait. I can assure you that such a situation is very unlikely when downstream legering. When legering across and upstream, I try to keep as much of the line out of the fast current as possible, allowing a loop of line to hang from the rod-tip into the slowest and steadiest water within immediate reach. The movement of line on a bite does allow a better chance of hooking the feeding barbel - in this respect I find the extra length of my rod critical. When fishing up or (rarely) downstream under my own bank, I use the extra length of the rod either to sit farther back, or to hold the line high for the reasons given above.

It will not have escaped the reader that earlier I categorically stated that 'sensitivity' comes high in my priorities. When tackle strength is at stake, the same holds, for far more often do I find a line of 5-6 lb breaking strain the means of contact between double-figure barbel and myself, than lines of 7 lb breaking strain or more. I know very good Thames anglers indeed, who still wait for their first 10 lb barbel, and in my opinion their failure stems mainly from the use of too powerful tackle. Of course, in some conditions, particularly heavy and coloured water, it is possible to step up the strength of line, as also it is in fading evening light, but the heavier the tackle I use, the markedly less my recorded success. Gwyn Williams, my constant angling companion, has landed a Thames barbel of 12 1/2 lb on the sort of tackle I recommend, to say nothing of rather a number of large 11 lb Thames fish, using the identical methods I suggest that the reader adopt. If the weight of our success leads you to adopt our methods, I anticipate that you will fish with advantage. Should you lose a record-breaking monster, we will share your sorrow and hope to better your luck.

To return to the advantages of upstream legering, it is significant that the bait can be more easily moved downstream in a natural manner. When this is not the case, I always strike off the bait, rather than parade it through the swim in a disturbing manner.

This is less easy with worms, but not impossible, for I snick them extremely lightly. Even so, I rarely catch fish in those Thames swims on this bait. No reasons or excuses can be offered here.

On the heavily fished reaches of the upper Thames,

I have a very distinct preference for smaller baits, which necessitate even more the finer, more sensitively-set tackle mentioned previously. Far and away the majority of our fish have fallen to smelly baits of the cheese-paste and sausage-meat variety - soft, very soft in both cases. When swims are encountered that are heavily fished, I like to avoid the use of the popular 'fish catching of the past' baits.

Gwyn Williams more or less sticks at soft sausage baits - and does rather better than theory suggests he should! These remarks are confined to the upper Thames let me add, for if I were to write of the Stour, Avon or Kennet, then a different tale would be told.

The brief mention made of swim-resting should not be passed too lightly, for in clear, low, or bright conditions, the habit of swim flogging is detrimental to likely sport. When conditions allow, we fish the most likely swims, at the most likely times (early or late) and leave them strictly alone outside these periods. In summer conditions it is so easy to make a start too soon, and delay the feeding of fish beyond that confounded, hour-after-sunset ban!

I rarely use float tackle in this evening period, as every available second is used in the area considered the most likely point of contact. Once cast, and checked for an untangled location, the bait is left for as long as nerves and confidence allow. One can 'work' an upstream swim, of course, but this is best done slowly, with long pauses between the short movements - leastways, that is my preference.

It is quite possible to use the tiniest of leads in apparently quite fast swims, if dense baits are used, and I am content to use the link method, which allows the addition of split shot leads as need dictates. While concerned with this tackle so proximate to a feeding fish, it is worth recording that any lead should be dulled or painted to imitate small stones. Unless the hook is completely covered it is clearly worth taking pains to avoid a shiny metal finish - the old adages of dull, reddish-brown hooks when using worms, white hooks for bread, gold for crust, etc., are bang-up-to-date in my eyes. Small baits suggest smaller hooks, but these must be strong - no point will be served by a painful recount of a personal experience; suffice to say, let them be strong.

Having re-read these lines, the writer is terribly conscious that in one sense he has failed to do justice to the subject of this chapter. While confident that the technical advice is basically sound, and likely to guide the aspiring angler along the right lines of successful big-barbel fishing, clearly I have failed to re-create the tremendous thrill of it all.

Of course, Gwyn and I have sat for hours, indeed days, without landing barbel. At times, no doubt, we have felt a little bored. Yet the impression generally left is one of satisfaction, amusement and sheer excitement. May I redress the balance a little by recounting just one day of sport that lingers in the mind's mirror.

It was autumn, not the golden Indian Summer so often enjoyed in this country by the non-barbel aspiring citizen, but a mild, wet end to an even wetter summer. When we left the dryness of Gwyn's car, we did not need to remind each other that hopes were running as high as the river, neither did we debate the swim of our choice. Gwyn simply insisted that I fish the 'high' water swim, for I had first introduced him to it, and characteristically, he selected the less-favoured run.

I was bothered by dace at almost every cast, until a lower station was selected where the swim ran a little deeper. No dace bites here. I was using worm at the time in the mistaken hope that in coloured water it would redeem its previous poor record. A change to sausage-meat immediately brought that slow nudge, often encountered when fishing across stream, which makes the chances of contact so high. That first reel-crushing run remains with me as vividly as any incident in my fishing life. It simply went, and I obediently followed, clasping a rod that did not thump as much as pull itself to the very water in a relentless downward curve. While vague notions of the subsequent fight fadedly peer through the gloom of distant time, almost equally clear is the image of Gwyn, with a smile on his Welsh face, eclipsed only by the look of open surprise on the mouth of the astonished Oxford barbel - or was it the other way round? Golden flanks and champagne fins looked enormous, even enfolded in the huge net. We cheered my first 11-pounder and breathlessly settled down, in the anti-climax of unlikely further hopes.

Gwyn bet me a pint that sport was finished, and lost - but that fish is virtually forgotten. An unselfish angling pal was finally convinced to join forces in the 'lucky' swim, only to lose a half-hooked fish as light finally faded.

# Fishing for Barbel

*Michael Shephard*

*'In summer he haunts the swiftest and shallowest Streams, where he lurks under the weeds, and works and routs with his Nose in the Sand like a Hog.'*
RICHARD BROOKES

Richard Brookes was writing of a fish which was far more numerous in this country in the middle of the eighteenth century, when *The Art of Angling* was first published, than it is now. Many rivers were shallower in those days, and where the water ran fast and clear it was over the shallower places, and there, as in streams today, the weeds flourished best. But the barbel no longer seeks shallow water specifically, except to scour and recover from spawning; the barbel seeks flowing water, but tends to choose the deeper places in the stream.

It was originally found in the Trent and Derwent and in a number of streams in Yorkshire, in the Thames and, I believe, in the Lea, but today there is little evidence of the extremely large shoals which once existed. On the other hand, since the fish was introduced to the Stour in Dorsetshire earlier this century it has flourished and has spread to the Lower Hampshire Avon, where, at Christchurch, big fish have consistently provided sport for many years.

It was at Christchurch that Roy Beddington landed a barbel of 16 lb 4 oz while fishing for salmon in 1931. It was during the close season for barbel, and the fish was returned, as so many big fish taken from that river have been returned, unharmed. I wish that an effort could be made to stock other seemingly suitable rivers with these fish, for they can provide a thrill which transcends the catching of most other coarse fish; they can also lie like logs, heedless of the anglers' baits - if tench are 'problematical' I have no word to describe the irritating vagaries of the barbel.

The fish has a prodigious appetite when it is feeding, and the appearance of a superabundance of food will often induce it to feed at times when fishing without ground-bait would fail. This takes us back to the days which died, I think with the First World War, when the baiting of barbel swims was carried out in a highly scientific way and thousands of lob-worms, wrapped in balls of clay or in bran and greaves, barley-meal or soaked bread, would be dropped into the river over a period of days to conjure up sport for a fishing-party at the weekend. Then, in punts tied to the stakes which marked the swim, the anglers would begin the day and end it with such a bag of barbel as we mere mortals can only imagine, but the veracity of which is preserved by faded photographs in inns and tackle shops along the Thames.

That the results of such fishing was not always a true reward for the effort is suggested by lines quoted in *Fishing and Fishers* in 1898:

*'Sing a song of Shepperton,*
*A bucketful of worms!*
*Four and twenty barbel wouldn't come to terms!*
*When the punt was fastened,*
*The barbel swam away.*
*Wasn't that a nice return for three half-crowns a day?'*

Frankly, I have not found that the proximity of a punt reacts on the nerves of the fish; they remain indolently below the boat, rub their sides against the anchor chains and steadfastly do nothing much else at all. But in order that they may accept my worms without any disturbing doubts as to why they appear, I have often fished the bait down on a long line to the shoal of fish which I have located; still they do nothing about my offering. Yet there are times when you can drop your anchors with a splash, throw in ground-bait and the bucket as well and the fish will feed hard and confidently. I do not advise this method, for the catching of barbel is a greater problem than legend would have us believe. Ground-baiting is one part of it today, the barbel the other.

After spawning on redds of sand or gravel in fast water (and this is why the fish so often seek out weirs where weirs are found) the barbel are often discovered in the latter part of May or early June recovering from their exertions in the fastest, most-aerated water available, rubbing themselves against the stones right under the fall of the weir or rolling like pigs in the sandy shallows at the end of the weir's scour. At such times it is said that the fish will feed on minnow and it is very possible that they do, but it is also said that minnow ceases to attract barbel after the first two or three weeks of the season, by which time the majority of the fish have returned to the deeper water, especially where the stream runs deep between the bank and some shallows. Sometimes you may find a fish or two in the fast water late in summer, and I can remember several occasions when barbel have been hooked there on worm in September. For serious fishing, however, the angler should seek out deeper and quieter places. Although barbel prefer a clean bed to lie on, they also enjoy the presence of weeds or old piles, a sunken tree or some other obstruction, and are capable of making good use of these when hooked. Of course, before you hook your barbel, you are usually fully aware of such dangers because already most of your new supply of hooks have found them and have remained.

As Richard Brookes told us, the fish rout about on the bottom for food, like pigs, and it is there that you must fish your bait, which may be a lump of bread and bran as big as a golf-ball, a lob-worm or its tail, a bunch of red worms or brandlings, cheese paste, maggots and occasionally hemp-seed or elderberry.

Generally speaking, lob-worms and the mixture of bread and bran are accepted as the best baits for barbel, but I have seen some good fish taken on maggots and many small ones by anglers fishing near the bottom for roach. Elderberry, however, was my own discovery (as far as I think myself to be the only angler who has caught a number of these fish on the bait). It was not intentional, but highly satisfactory, and the way of it was this.

I had never caught a barbel, but had hooked them and had seen them hooked during August and September that year. Knowing where the fish were, two of us decided to try for them on Sunday at the beginning of October, and it was for that reason that I waited impatiently for the last of the football results in the office of the provincial newspaper for which I worked. By half-past six I was home, and by seven, after a hasty meal, the rods and baskets, a landing-net and a gaff (in case of a pike), a bucket of stale bread, a bag of bran and a smaller bag of greaves, a small sack of lob-worms in moss and Jack and I were in the car heading for Oxford and beyond. By eight-thirty we were drinking a cup of tea in a little café near the bridge and describing to the owner the shape and size of the fish which we would show him on our return. Reaching Clifton Hampden we found, below the Bridge House, a luxurious tent with two beds made up for us and the fishing punt ready below the willows, only twenty feet away.

After stowing our gear in the punt, the rods up and ready, we went to sleep, and asleep we remained through the raucous call of the alarm until the first light of morning awoke us to mutual reproach and disgust, for the weir lay a long way up-stream, and we had intended to be there and fishing as soon as it was light enough to see our floats. Instead we were fishing by eight o'clock.

In those days there was a shallow lying across the

river some forty yards from the weir, and round it the water had kept open a deep channel under each bank. It was the site of an old weir, we were told, and that accounted for the presence of the stumps of piles which lay below us firmly embedded in the sand. Here, only a month earlier, another friend had hooked and almost landed a large barbel, only to have it foul the cast round one of the chains which held the punt in position.

We anchored our boat about twenty yards above the narrow channel in which the fish lay. Our ground-bait had been thrown in as gently as possible, and behind it we allowed a worm to drift down on the current, every now and then. In those days I had not discovered the efficacy of bran and bread as bait (ground-bait, yes), and we fished exclusively with lob-worms. Almost as soon as we had started, Jack's float dipped and was drawn slowly down a fraction of an inch to dive under with a suddenness typical of a barbel; tightening, he dragged a diminutive daddy-ruffe to the surface. And so for three hours we fished on, and caught, it seemed, every ruffe, every gudgeon and every tiny perch which swam in the weir-pool, and each one bit like a barbel, so that, although gradually dwindling, our hopes remained high for some time. By eleven o'clock the sun had become so hot and our seats so cramped that we decided to stretch our legs and potter about until later in the day, when the barbel *might* come on.

However, we were anxious not to miss the barbel, and settled down to fish for roach from the bank above the swim we had baited. We used our big rods (twelve feet of whole cane and built cane top), our 2x casts, but No. 14 hooks in place of the No. 8 hooks on which we had impaled our lob-worms. We fished with hemp-seed and with elderberries, and caught many small roach.

I had brought with me my father's little roach-rod which weighed $3^{1}/_{2}$ - 4 oz, and, growing impatient, I put it up with its light line, a cast of 5x and a No. 12 hook and wandered off to fish in the weir while Jack stayed behind to catch small roach and to watch my big rod, which was fishing a worm on the bottom.

About some things that day my memory is a little hazy, but I do remember being broken by something big in the weir and returning to put on a new cast. I found that Jack was catching some slightly bigger roach, and joined him, fishing my elderberry deeper and deeper in search of a really big one. The inevitable happened as my hook dragged over the bottom; the float went under, and I broke in tightening on what was by no means a certain bite. When this happened a second time I felt sure that I must be striking one of the piles, and the third time, when I lifted my rod more gently and was held fast, and Jack said gloomily, "Bottom?" the bottom moved. Slowly, inexorably, it took line with it until there was nothing but a still, dead strain, and I knew that the fish had tied me up on some obstruction. Obviously it was a barbel, and not two piles?

We were excited, to say the least, and Jack lengthened his cast to fish the bottom as well, while I put another worm on my big rod and continued to fish with elderberry with the little one. And it was not long before I was into another fish.

If there was any exaggeration about that battle it was in the behaviour of the little rod, which was bent as no rod of its kind should be. After a sullen movement around on the bottom of the channel, the fish began a run which developed from something rather like the first downward rush of a chub to the long run of a salmon, but, of course, not so fast. Still, it was fast enough for me, and as the barbel ran over the gently ascending gravel bank towards the shallows the line cut through the water and the reel sang. What would have happened had I been using the longer, more powerful rod, with its 8 lb breaking strain line and 2x cast, I do not know; but with that fairy wand in my hand and a line of gossamer and cast even finer, there was nothing to do but keep the rod upright and allow the reel to sing. The reel itself was an old one, and probably needed a drop of oil, but my barbel obviously believed, as did the schoolmaster, that 'little birds which can sing, but which will not sing, must be made to sing'.

It sang until a huge wave (the word is purely proportionate to the occasion - it seemed huge) followed a great fish over those shallows where the fry leaped from the water to avoid yet another of the predations to which they had become accustomed, living as they did in the proximity of trout, perch, pike, eels and chub. Then the fish was dropping into the deep water of the far channel - water edged by reeds and weed-beds. My line was almost out, for there was only fifty yards in all upon the reel when I first put the rod up. The speed of the run slackening, the fish moved solid and unstoppable towards the deepest part of the weir, and there (perhaps the slight strain of the arched rod, the strength of the stream against the line and the fish itself began to tell) it started to bore and roll on the bed of the river below twenty feet of water. Somehow, during those next few minutes I managed to exercise some little control over the fish, and regained some line in case a fresh burst of energy forced me to give something away. I was happy; I had been happy from the start, but now there was that happiness which comes after sudden, straining excitement, when one knows that at least the fish is firmly hooked and that so far everything has held together. Yet, apart from a vague shape as it crossed the shallows, I had not seen the fish and had no idea of its size. About ten minutes later the barbel did show, and, with the fish fighting just as strongly but more sullenly, I began to conquer it.

Gradually my reel clicked over and the fish moved nearer, only to bore down towards the bottom and take back a little of the line I had gained; then, with a sudden rush along the bottom, it was almost below me in the deep water under my bank, and heading for the sanctuary which the old piles of its home afforded. It was the one moment when I just had to hold that fish away from trouble . . . Well, somehow everything sustained the strain, and the fish checked its run and continued to bore. Finally I had it swimming just below the surface on a short line, and Jack had scrambled down the steep bank with the net; the net was in the water, the fish was drifting over it - a great bar of brown and olive-green - and the time had come to rejoice. But this was one of those moments when you learn never to count a kettle of fish until you have first boiled the kettle - the landing-net screwed into a metal ferrule on the end of a long handle, and that ferrule, after years of neglect, was corroded, weakened. As the weight of the fish was felt, the metal split and the net, fish and all fell back into the water with a splash. For a moment the fish swam in the net, and then, fortunately, came free and seemed to regain energy from the shock. I soon had him under control again, and this time brought him to the bank ready for the gaff, which I had somehow passed down to Jack. But Jack's position was precarious on the steep side of the bank, and as he - the veteran of many expeditions after pike - moved to bring the sharp steel point to the fish he slipped and the lunging gaff just missed my cast.

Away went the fish again - slowly, it is true - and I began to wonder what was to happen next, when help came in the form of another angler, who, seeing my plight, had crossed the weir from his own barbel-fishing and had brought with him a large net on a handle of solid strength.

Once again I brought my fish to the bank, and in a moment he was on it to be admired, to be weighed and admired again. Incidentally, he weighed 9½ lb - the biggest barbel I have ever caught, as well as the first.

It is interesting to note that in the Thames, barbel of

10 lb and over are rare; I remember Dick Gower telling me, when I showed him my fish that evening, that at one time three fishermen regularly baited that weir pool in an attempt to catch a fish of 10 lb and, although they caught many fish of 9 lb, they never achieved their ambition.

On the Hampshire Avon, however, 10-pounders are caught fairly often, and I think this points to the theory that water conditions and supply of food do affect the average top weight of fish taken from any water; we know it to be fact, not theory, in the case of trout and of roach and carp, and I suggest that it is equally true of all fish that are not migratory.

What gives a river its reputation of being a 'big-fish river' where salmon are concerned I do not know, except that more big salmon are caught in such a river than in others; why those salmon are bigger, when they all feed and grow in the sea, has yet to be discovered. I think that it is also true that barbel taken from rivers other than the Avon and the Thames tend to run to a smaller average weight.

The second fish I caught that day was also a good one for the Thames - 7¹/₄ lb - but would not have been considered takeable on the Avon. The third fish, and the last that day, weighed 5 lb - not too bad for the Thames, but insignificant in the Avon. I caught all three within the space of an hour, after which not another barbel was hooked, although we fished until it was too dark to see. Another strange thing was the way in which I had the bites and hooked the fish while Jack, fishing the same swim, never caught anything but roach on his elderberry. Was it, I wonder, anything to do with my 5x as opposed to his 3x? I do not think so, and I have experienced the same inexplicable selection of Fate when fishing with other anglers for other fish: the evening when my father caught seven good bream from the swim we were sharing, and I did not have a bite, yet I was using exactly the same tackle and the same bait and our floats were often lying within inches of each other; the hot August afternoon when I managed to land five fair carp while my two companions in the boat, fishing more or less in the same place with the same bait and the same tackle, failed to connect with a single fish; and only the other day, when fishing with an American friend over communal ground-bait in a communal swim, I did not have a bite, although he had fish after fish take his bait over a period of two hours. Surely Fate does play a hand? I have yet to find another reason, as I explain in a later chapter.

The first barbel-fishing I did after the war was in 1947, also October, when I visited Christchurch to talk to local anglers about pollution. With that hospitality which seems to have become a tradition of angling, and which I have found among anglers wherever I have met them, it was arranged that I should have a morning on the Avon, and I was lucky enough to be shown the bounds by J. B. Parkinson. Since I had said how keen I was to try for one of the big barbel for which the Royalty water has become renowned, he fixed me up with bait, ground-bait and rod and line.

It was a glorious day, a morning of autumn frost followed by the freshness and warmth of a late summer's sun. But the river was fairly full and the stream was running fast, bringing with it rafts of floating weed as a result of cutting operations farther upstream - often a curse on such rivers in the autumn, but very necessary. Because of the current it was also necessary to ledger, and the tackle Parkinson had fixed up for me was a running shot fixed about three feet above the hook.

He explained that in the swim I was to fish the barbel lay in the deep water close under the campsheathing of my bank. He also did his best to teach me a form of casting with which I was not at that time familiar and which even today I have not fully mastered. With the rod in the right hand, you make a back-hand cast across the body, swinging the bait out in the required direction and at the same time pulling line off the reel with sufficient power of the left wrist and arm to produce an even supply of line to follow the weight of the ledger tackle and bait without checking its flight or causing an over-run. In this way the bait reached the surface about half-way across the river, where it began to sink, and was carried round and down to the position which it was intended to fish.

We were using a mixture of bread and bran as bait, and for that reason a much smoother cast was needed than with worms or maggots; also a lump of bread-and-bran mixture was squeezed round the ledger lead as ground-bait, and it was necessary that no sudden jerk in the flight of the lead or heavy arrival on the surface should displace it or loosen it if it was to reach the bed of the river up-stream of the hook-bait.

Parkinson made the first cast and, once satisfied that the bait was in the right place, handed the rod to me. With such a strength of current, I had to fish a tight line on which any bite would be felt - no time or place for an 'Idle Jack'! I was told that if the barbel were going to bite at all it would not be long before they did so, and very soon I noticed a trembling sensation greater than that caused by the passage of water past my line; then there was a steady drag against the rod-top, as though a submerged piece of drifting weed was pulling on the line.

But my guide told me that it was a barbel investigating the bait, sucking it . . . "Well, when do I strike?" I asked. "When it takes properly it'll bang your rod-top really hard." Unfortunately, when the bang came it took me by surprise, and I had to bait up again. Once more I felt that prolonged trembling and a slight draw on the line, and I gave the rod to Parkinson, who crouched beside me. The bang came, and as I saw the rod-top suddenly pulled down, it was lifted by the fisherman, and the barbel was on. A typically powerful but slow run against the stream, and then the fish turned and went down with the current, so that Parkinson was forced to follow it along the bank in a hurry.

But the fight in that strong current belied the size of the fish, and I eventually netted a beautifully conditioned barbel of about 5lb. Unhooked, it was returned to the water.

This has been a general review of barbel-fishing - one form of fishing of which I have not had enough experience to become either instructional or, thank Heavens, dogmatic, but there is one essential of barbel-fishing upon which I can dwell with a certain amount of authority - the matter of worms, which provide bait.

I have been in more or less constant pursuit of worms since I was a lad. At first it was a quest for lug-worms and rag-worms on the seashore below the level of the high tide; later it became a hunt for land-worms of every kind - red-worms, brandlings, marsh-worms and the large blue-nosed lob-worm of the lawn and the vegetable garden. Anyone who has ever dug a patch of garden will know that with every spit of earth there comes a small harvest of worms; but anyone who is an angler and bent upon the task of finding bait for fish will know that many spits of earth must be turned before enough worms have been obtained. Furthermore, worms straight from the earth are not what are needed for good fishing.

Fish have a taste for such things, if nothing else, and they require worms which are fresh and clean and lively. Therefore, you must obtain your worms and keep them in such a way as will preserve them fresh for fishing, harden them for the hook and cleanse them of any dirt or mud.

But let us first consider the provision of worms, and reserve our subsequent treatment of them. Red-worms are best obtained by leaving old sacks or pieces of board on the ground in quiet and damp parts of the garden; rotting vegetation will also attract these worms, and it is well if you can arrange for a small compost-heap in some quiet corner. After leaving your worm-trap for a week or more, you may visit it at intervals of a day or two and pick up whatever you find beneath it, but in hot, dry weather it is best to dampen the board, sacking or compost and the ground surrounding it at regular intervals. Your marsh-worms may be obtained in much the same way by placing traps in the drier parts of swampy ground or by digging there, lifting up roots of rough grass and rush and turning over any decomposing matter you may come across. A very similar and probably more suitable bait may be obtained by digging close to the water and below water level, lifting the bottom of the river in shallow places - a natural, lively, long-living worm which toughens well under the same treatment which I shall prescribe for the rest of the worm tribe.

Before turning to this treatment, however, I must mention the brandling and the lob-worm. The brandling - tiger-striped, yellow-juiced and evil-smelling at first - is the produce pure and simple of the dung-heap, and the older the foundation of that heap the more worms you will find; it is no good dumping a load of dung and expecting to find worms in it within a short time. Your manure-heap must be well established, and I have yet to find any better than horse manure and straw - a dying commodity, which often makes the supply of brandlings too small to satisfy the demand. For the tench fisherman, at least a knowledge of local manure-heaps is almost as necessary as the knowledge of tench-waters.

However, the lob-worm is the main subject for our consideration at the moment, for it is an excellent bait for barbel, bream, carp, roach, eels, tench, chub, salmon and sea-trout. You can dig your lob-worms if you want to break your back (imagine digging four or five thousand), but the best way of building up a store is to pick them off a lawn by the light of a torch. This is back-breaking work enough, but as soon as you have mastered the knack of stalking your worm, gripping it behind the head - somewhere about the fifth or sixth segment - resisting its immediate and elastic withdrawal backwards into its hole, and then pulling it out without breaking it, you will be able to pick up half-a-dozen worms in a minute. Naturally, to get a good supply of worms, just as a good supply of pheasants, the conditions must be right and you must foster them. The lob-worm has been called 'night-crawler', 'dew-worm', because under cover of darkness it emerges from its hole to bask in the dew- or rain-soaked grass, to mate and, for all I know, play; it also feeds, pulling grass and other vegetation backwards into its hole. But to get as many worms as possible on the surface the condition of your lawn must be right, and it may be necessary to soak the ground thoroughly in times of drought.

The sport of picking up worms is secondary only to catching fish on them, and for the newcomer at a hotel I can honestly say that there is no finer way of breaking the first-night tension in the lounge and making new friends than by watching the evening arrive and going out into the night to prowl about with a torch on the lawn. "What's he lost?" someone asks. "I don't know . . . " answers another, and within seconds all attention is focused on the half-bent figure who moves murkily about in the gloom beyond the window-panes. "Trying to get in first with the mushrooms," announces a wag, and then, unable to stand the strain any longer, he goes out on to the lawn and stands watching for a moment or two before asking point-blank, "Oh . . . er . . . excuse me butting in, old man, but what on earth are you looking for?" Or perhaps the lonely blonde, with all the natural sympathy of one who has herself lost a diamond ring, emerges to ask, "Can I help you find it?"

Tom, Dick or Hermione - tinker, tailor, fisherman or philatelist it does not matter . . . sooner or later they must be introduced to this new form of entertainment and join in. You can say goodbye to the worms, but there is a lot of fun to be had out of it - and I know, for I have broken the ice myself. But, seriously, it is quite the best way to catch your worms, although there are others. You can force a garden fork into the lawn and strum the handle as you would the strings of a double bass. The worms come to the surface. You can, I am told, pour a solution of mustard and water into the holes of the worms and the worms will come to the surface; but, however you obtain them, you must treat your captives gently and with the greatest care, for there is nothing more liable to drive fish from your hook than a battered, stinking, half-dead worm, and nothing deteriorates, dies and then decomposes more quickly than a worm which has been mishandled or kept without proper care.

If you imagine that you will pick up all the worms you need for barbel-fishing in one night, disabuse yourself: you will not. I have personally caught and counted just over one thousand worms, but I was unable to go fishing next day as a result of it. No, you must build up a good stock by gradual stages, by regular onslaughts on the lawn, by a series of concerts on the fork handle or by constant doses of the mustard potion. And as you build up your supply you must watch your stock carefully. Mr Coombe Richards gives some excellent advice on the care of worms in his book *Informative Fishing*, and I cannot better it, although I can condense his advice and mix it with my own.

You can keep a large number of worms in a small space just so long as they are protected from too much moisture, too much heat and too much cold. They react to heat very quickly, and die equally easily if bitten by frost. Also they are very quickly affected by (yes, believe it) dirt, and as they are likely to foul their nest, especially in the first few hours after their removal from their natural environment, great care must be taken to ensure that their new home is kept clean. I must make it quite clear now that there is very little point in anyone trying to build up a store of worms unless he is willing to look after those worms with as much regular attention as he would give to his well-kept ferrets.

The first thing to do with your fresh-caught worms is to allow them to scour themselves, and this is done by putting them in moss.

I suggest that you should prepare two containers - one for fresh-caught worms and the other as the store to which worms should be transferred after three or four days' scouring. Dig a pit into which a fairly solid box will fit easily, and put a layer of about three inches of silver sand in the bottom. Your box should be equipped with drainage holes in the bottom, and these can be covered by wire gauze or perforated zinc to avoid a loss of any worms which escape from the sack in which they are kept.

Put a layer of straw or moss in the bottom of the box, and fill a sack (as large as you require, but strong and closely knit) with fresh *dry* moss. Put your worms, once scoured, in this, and sprinkle a small amount of water on to the top of the sack when you have placed it in the box.

Now make a fairly flat palliasse by stuffing a second sack with straw, and lay this over the top of the one containing the worms - it acts as an insulator against both heat and cold, and in winter a similar insulator should be tucked in round the sides of the box. Place a board over the top of the box or fit it with a lid. Your main store is now complete, and you must prepare a similar one on smaller lines to take each night's catch until they have scoured in the moss for four or five days. Mr Coombe Richards tells us that he uses 'two medium- to large-sized earthenware flower-pots, with corks in the holes in the bottom' and, although I have never used these - one inverted on top of the other - I imagine that they must be very satisfactory as long as the same precautions are taken against heat and frost.

But do not imagine that it ends with the provision of a home; having built up a welfare state for the creatures, you have taken on, besides providing housing, the responsibility for their health and their feeding. Health is maintained by a daily inspection of the container, the removal of any dead or weakly worms, turning the sack upside down so that the worms will work back through the moss from the top, instead of continuing to lie all day in a congested, greasy bundle on the bottom, damping the moss and feeding its inhabitants. This last you can do by mixing milk or ale with the damping water, but only a little. Mr Richards keeps his main store in a large box, too, but he keeps them in mould, and feeds them on the sort of vegetable left-overs from the kitchen which one saves for pigs or chickens. Red-worms and brandlings do well on such food, but lob-worms prefer fresh grass and leaves. However, I have found that the worms do equally well in moss with food added and removed before it decomposes too much; in fact, I have kept worms for several weeks in a box in which they lay between two sacks - damp, of course. Every few days the sacks would be changed for new ones and the soiled ones sluiced down, dried and used again at the next change-over. I have also found this to work well with both rag-worms and lug-worms.

Of course, even with care you may have bad luck, and I have lost hundreds of worms in a day for no apparent reason. Remember that worms are not two-a-penny, but a penny apiece today!

I hope that this diversion from the subject of barbel has not seemed out of place. Worms are important to most fishermen at some time or another, and it is as well to use the best when that time comes.

## The Barbel

*Patrick Chalmers*

*The trout his ambush keeps Crafty and strong,*
*in Pangbourne's eddying pools, But patient still in Marlow deeps*
*For the shy barbel wait expectant fools.*
ANON.

The barbel is really a carp, or so the experts say. He owes his name, after the Bluebeard mode, to the four minute *feelers*, the little, one inch long, beards which impend two from his upper lip and two from the angles of his rather gross mouth. These four little beards are, so the experts say once more, the most sensitive little indicators in the world. The lurking mollusc, shrimp or water snail, has no chance against them, it is discovered at once and is the barbel's principal *plat* when the silk-weed is not up for him to pasture upon.

The barbel is the most important, the truest and the most stubborn, of the Thames fishes. He is indigenous here, and from Thames he has gone to stock Stour and

Avon, who now boast him in quantity and personal bulk. He grows to a great size, fifteen-pound barbel if not common upon the bank, or in the punt, are at least reasonably plentiful in the middle reaches of the river and I do verily believe that this weight may occasionally be exceeded by five pounds or more. These mighty fellows are met with in May by the trout angler who fishes with a live minnow and a little too much weight. For the barbel is a bottom feeder and a more or less omnivorous one, and minnows and little fish are all in the menu. He will not, however, hunt them as a trout or a pike does, yet he will accept them as and when they occur. The trout-angler's minnow will seem just the easy thing. The barbel will take it and, if he does not smash the whole fine outfit, he will in due course be landed and returned carefully to the Thames since he is, till June 15th, unseasonable and sacrosanct.

The biggest barbel that I have ever heard of came about as above. The angler, an expert and knowledgeable angler, was fishing in the open river above Sonning. A very large trout had been located in an eddy between there and Caversham. The state of the weather and the water gave the angler cause to think that the trout would be well down in the deep of the 'lie'. He therefore pinched on another lead or two and presently sat down in the May sunshine, his cork forty yards away, his finger on the undressed silk line. In the angler's boat were two passengers, professional fishermen taking a busman's holiday and studying the methods of the most renowned of Thames amateurs.

Presently a great fish was hooked. It was soon obvious to all that here was no trout but a most prodigious barbel. The angler played it for twenty minutes and then, anxious to return to his legitimate excuse, he broke the fine trace all a-purpose. During the play the fish had been seen, huge, chocolate-brown, white-bellied, and the consensus of sober opinion was that the scale-breaking monster would weigh between twenty and twenty-three pounds. But the trout never materialised and the fisherman regrets to this day that he did not land the barbel and ascertain its actual bulk before returning it to the river. I regret this too but I am satisfied that the poundage would have proved up to estimate.

Barbel spawn in mid-May and it is the most fascinating sight on all Thames to see them, a week or two later, rejoicing that about 25,000 little barbels a-piece have been born to them. Before the Conservancy deepened Goring weir pool and destroyed, with their dredgers and drogues, the first fine rapture of its river beauty, there was no better place to see the barbel in madcap mood than from the old wooden road-bridge. The bridge has gone too but it was a pleasant bridge to lean upon as you went to Streatley. There you would see the shoals of big barbel pushing and rolling on the golden gravels. Golden-brown fish, you would see, in golden-brown water flecked with sunshine and the green shadows of the bulrush beds that thrust up in a panoply of green spears out of shallow middle stream. Blue-and-white sky, swifts and swallows to swoop and to soar, speeding wings and speeding water - what summers used to be in Berkshire once!

These Goring barbel always seemed to be, as they porpoise-rolled and leapt and turned over and over, of a lighter shade than the barbel that I first knew in Thames. These were the barbel of Shiplake and Marlow and my memories are of long chocolate-brown backs, bronze-shaded upon and shadowed with jade and olive. But I have no doubt that barbel are as chameleon as trout are, as all fish are, and that they take their colour from their environment and the river-pools in which they swim.

Sometimes enormous shoals of barbel may be seen. Early one morning in the miracle summer of 1911 I looked over a garden wall into the fine water and the fan-out of what the drought had left of Whitchurch weir pool. I saw a dark cloud of backs, backs some so long that I hesitate to speak of them and to compare them in length to dining-room tables. But I saw big backs, medium backs, and backs of mere four-pounders.

I had in my hand a little rod and it was up and baited with a small red worm, for I wanted to catch some gudgeon. The barbel had not seen me and, hidden, I dropped my tackle over the wall. I was rewarded by hooking something like a torpedo that, moving up the pool, smashed me forthwith. Nothing makes a man feel more impotent than to hook a big barbel on a tiny rod. And a barbel is a terrific fighter. His fins are large and strong, his 'streamy' lines indicate tremendous power and a turn of real speed. Nothing gives you a better idea of this fish's strength than to see, in summer, a shoal of barbel lying, nose against the river, in the very green-and-white rush of Thames as he drives headlong through one of his sluices. There will be eight or nine great fish, shoulder to golden shoulder, sometimes sinking into the mysteries, sometimes ascending till the angles of big forked tails show above the river. Motionless will they be otherwise and, always, keeping their vantage against the full weight of water with splendid ease and power.

I, when first I came to Thames, knew nothing of his

coarse fishes and less of his trout, though of the last I had heard rumours. I came from salmon river and fly-rods, I came from waters where the ousel and the ring-ousel go from boulder to splashed boulder and where the trout go four to the pound, perhaps, three to the pound if you're lucky.

My father, 'hard by the thundering Spey', said, when told that I was about to pitch my tent upon Thames-side, "There are trout in the Thames; not only that but once I took one out of it." He said that about 1860 he had been at a tutor's near Boveney. He walked with a contemporary by the river. There was a punt tied to the bank below the weir. In the punt was a rod in readiness for use even to a live bleak that, upon the hook, swam in the cool current. The owner of this punt and its appurtenances had just gone to *The Prince Regent* to get a glass of ginger ale.

The two boys got into the punt and the one, something of a waterman, punted upstream. The other threw the bait out. It was instantly seized and a four-pound trout was landed. A peep into the well showed a supply of bait. So, the rightful angler still absent, a fresh bait was put on and the same cast essayed. Once more it was taken, this time by a trout estimated to be twice, if not thrice, as big as the first. It jumped. It tore the line out in one long run into the white water.

Thither the puntsman was not expert enough to follow it. The punt went down-stream, in fact, while the trout went up. The line parted with a *ping*; the rightful angler stood on the bank gesticulating and scandalously blasphemous.

But he was a good sort, for he presently gave the boys the trout that they had caught and confessed that he himself had been fishing Boveney for a week and had had, during that time, 'never a bloody nibble'.

So I knew a little of Thames trout before I knew Thames, by whom I walked for the first time upon a May afternoon. On the footbridge at Marsh I stopped and looked into the clear water. Upon the gravel bottom and only a few yards from where I stood were three large fish, four pounds, five pounds perhaps. "Trout," said I.

And as I spoke, from over against the mill, another fish, darkly golden, leapt from bright water into blue air and fell back with a sounding splash. If the three fish on the shallow were big what sort of an outsize in trout was this? Twelve pounds if he was an ounce. And I marvelled and would have run home for a rod had I had one and known how to use it on a Thames trout.

It took me a month to learn the difference between a trout and a barbel. Where I came from trout were brown fish of a similar brown to the great fellow that had jumped under the mill's wall. So a mistake was excusable, given that a trout *could* be so splendid a fish and prodigious.

But I was soon to be reminded that the caudal fin, or tail, of a trout is square. And that that of the barbel, and of all the coarse fish except the tench, except the eel, is forked like Jove's lightnings or the tongues of asps. And that the trout in Thames is nearly always a silvery fish, silver and blue and dotted on with sable in his prime; with, possibly, a red spot or so as he ages or goes out of condition. Nearly always is this so. A dark-coloured trout is, it is safe to say, either out of condition or old. Or both these sad things at once. Yet not always, for I once caught a fine, shapely trout that weighed eight pounds and he was as brown as a berry.

And I learnt that, when a trout springs out of the water, which he often does in May and June, he comes out head first, hangs a moment quivering in air, and then drops back tail first. A barbel springs up in similar style but he, at apogee, turns over neatly in air and goes home again as head first as he came.

So now that you know a little of barbel let us try to catch one. The common form of barbelling on the Thames is by bottom fishing, or legering. Your success in the art is the most uncertain thing in all angling. The barbel is the most capricious fish that swims. Carp? Trout? Oh, don't be ridiculous. In the Thames your trout will not be so many and your carp fewer still. But neither trout nor carp goes flauntingly and in great shoals, schools or congregations. But this is how the barbel goes; he goes profusely and yet remains the most unfacile of all the fish.

You may leger in a baited or an unbaited swim. If you ask me which way is the more likely to provide sport I will answer that I do not know. But if you ask what a swim is, it is the name given to any particular piece of water where a shoal of barbel may be working.

In the Thames, swims are gravel bottomed almost invariably. The shoals, in early and middle summer, are, as we have seen, on the shallows at the tails of weir-pools and mill-races. As the summer advances they drop back, or push up, into deeper water. But they will not go very far away and may be located easily enough by the splashing brown-and-white, acrobatic turns in which the barbel betrays himself. In the main river the same somersaults may guide you if you will watch for them, dropping quietly downstream at morning or in the swift-haunted dusk.

Having found your swim the next thing is to fish it. If you are going to bait it first, you will require worms. How many? Five thousand, my lad, five thousand lobworms at, I think, eight shillings a thousand and cheap too considering that these lobs must be hand-caught and cannot be bred in captivity, as if they were lions or meal-worms.

The easiest way of baiting a swim is to engage a professional fisherman to bait it for you. You will pay him for his time and for, of course, the worms which he will get from Nottingham. I do not know why lobworms come from Nottingham but they do. The fisherman will drop the worms into the swim at sunrise and with incantations. He will do this for two days before you fish and he will reserve a thousand of the worms for you to use upon your hook or to throw in, as largesse, if the fun slackens on the morning on which you come out. He will make dumplings of clay and fill them with worms and drop them into the swim. Any fishing book will tell you how these clay worm-puddings are made. Or he may prefer to use weighted, brown paper bags instead of the clay puddings. In this case, before their committal to the deep, he tears off the bottom corners of the bags so that 'the worms they creep in and the worms they creep out', and the bags fill with Thames water and sink. It is all very expensive and elaborate but the barbel is an expensive and elaborate fish. But he can be done a little cheaper if you use graves from the butcher instead of lobs. I am not quite sure what part of the internal arrangements of a sheep is graves but it is procurable by that name. Worms and graves, then, are the barbel's morbid preferences.

And, as I have said, there are excellent books to tell you how a barbel swim may best be baited and I have nothing new or helpful to add to them. And so, in the grey of a late August morning, you will go to your sport. You will *not* find another fishing the swim that you have baited because Thames fishermen are sportsmen and they understand that a ryepeck, standing like a pinnacle in the wilderness, means that a brother has proprietary rights to the pitch it implies.

You will anchor your boat some twenty yards from where you are to fish. The commonplace rod is the rod that we have up and ready. I use the Nottingham reel on it and, personally, I use the same undressed line with a rub of vaseline thereon. There is no cheerful float to enliven leger-fishing.

The leger I will briefly describe but it can be bought at any tackle-maker's - where, by the way, the worms necessary to it can also be ordered. The leger consists of two foot of salmon gut. Following on the gut is a foot of gimp. To slide upon the gimp is a perforated lead weight. To prevent this lead slipping down to the hook there is at the lower end of the gimp a stop-shot. Next to the stop-shot comes another foot and a half of gut, then a swivel and then the single, fairly big, bait hook. And that's your leger.

Thread now a worm on to the hook; tail first is the approved fashion. Barbel are said, I do not know by whom, to pick up the worm always by the tail. Swing out the bait gently upon the free reel. When your touch tells you that the lead is upon the bottom, tighten the line until you hold it tautly and in direct communication with the bait. Throw in a few worms as an inducement and now sit down and be as patient as possible, and as wide-awake.

The rod should be held low, the point may almost be on the water. This because it is necessary that the angler should recognise, forthwith, the first symptoms of a bite. When this tiny pull comes to you, let go about six inches of line which you will be holding loose and ready. Then hold tight and strike firmly but not furiously.

I have said that the barbel is a terrific fighter. But he is not a spectacular one. A barbel is not netted after the tenth leap as though he were a spring grilse below Banchory. A barbel does not take fifty yards fairly off the reel line in his first rush; neither a trout is he nor a sea-trout. But he is as strong as a cart horse and his are the staying powers of a social bore. He fights deep down and he goes on fighting. The floors of Thames are his home, and if he can rub out your hold of him thereon or break you in his labyrinths of weed and lily stalks, why, he most certainly will. Weight for weight, I do not hesitate to say that a barbel takes a longer time to kill than does a trout or a pike. Or even a salmon.

So strike him firmly but not to the breaking point. It is one of the several extraordinary things about this extraordinary fish that he will continue to use a swim and feed with equanimity upon your worm dumplings the while you fight a dozen or so of his brothers to the death before his very eyes. And yet do one of the brethren beat you - well, a barbel with a foot of fine gut sticking out of his mouth will stampede the shoal like a breakaway of tups.

It is a wonderful thing to see a school treat of barbel enjoying the worm dumplings of their benefactor. If you are fortunate enough to have found and baited a swim in the open river, where some convenience of bank or willow bough allows you to lie secretly and look down into ten feet of clear water, such a show may sometimes be vouchsafed you.

You will see your clay puddings festooned with the pink tails of lobs. You will see the dark cloud of fish. This cloud will taper into a sort of triangle, the apex of which is nearest to the treat. The leading barbel will help himself to one worm. He will then go about abruptly to resume his place once more at the base of the triangle while, in rotation, the others duly take their turns.

But the baiting of a swim is a speculation. It is a thing to do once in a lifetime, or twice. If it comes off and you catch 200 lb weight of barbel in a twelve hours' sitting, you may from henceforth rest on your honours, for so red a letter day will not occur again. If you catch a small perch and one unsizeable barbel you will be equally content to let the experience be your teacher.

To bait a swim and fish it for two days will cost the average angler who must buy his lobs and employ a fisherman between four and five pounds. More than that if travelling and hotels have to be budgeted for.

Once, for the entertainment of a guest, I employed Walter Coster to bait a swim for me at Marlow. No one could have done it better than he. Worms were no object to us, we had lobs by the thousand. Our pitch was the choicest in Marlow's lovely pool and, early and late, we fished it for two days. Our bag was a small eel and a half-pound chub.

To bait then or not to bait? I think on the whole not to. Go to your swim with a thousand worms.

Throw a couple of hundred in, bread upon the waters, before you begin to put your rod together and then another couple of hundred, and possibly they shall return to you, presently, buttered of barbel.

Lobs too are not the barbel's natural food, possibly he never sees a lob throughout the season except one with a catch to it. So his taste in this direction must be cultivated and this may often be a longer task than the two or three days we devote to the baiting up of a swim. Whereas he may succumb at once to the novelty of the occasional and unexpected pinkiness that wriggles upon the golden river-floors.

Another objection that I have to the baited swim, especially the baited swim in the August weir pool, is that it attracts, too often, the trout of the entire neighbourhood. The Conservancy forbids the fishing for trout with worm but it allows the retention of a sizeable trout taken upon the worm intended for his coarser cousins. It is a sorry thing to see an aristocrat killed in such a way. And the more unsizeable the trout the greater is the likelihood that he will defeat the best of intentions and die or ever the extraction of the leger hook is accomplished. I think, with all the fishing books, that when a caught fish is to be returned to the river and the hook has been over well taken, no attempt at extraction should be made. A nip of the scissors to sever the gut, a short holding of the invalid's head to current and a trust in Father Thames that he, and the acids in the patient's own blood, will get rid of the barb in no time, and the trout may hopefully be seen to go.

Were I a Conservator of Thames I think that I would forbid worm fishing of any kind in the weir pools. If barbel swims must be baited within the pools let the method be graves, for of graves, the economical, a trout thinks small beer. And it is in summer that the trout come into the pools after the fry. And it is in high summer and late that the barbel swim is baited.

For in winter the barbel is a slugabed. Under rafts, boat-houses and landing stages, in the seclusion of the deepest holes and river corners that he can find, there, packed like the partridges, he hibernates. But not entirely, for a mild day will bring him out to take, and smash the tackle to smithereens, the roach-poler's hemp seed or his gentle.

So the usual way to catch Thames barbel is on the leger. But there are other methods, for the barbel is capable of anything from a grain of hemp seed to a fairly large live gudgeon. And many a good fish has been caught on a minnow, especially in late June or early July.

Take the live-bait rod, the ten-foot, thirty-five-year-old split-cane that I told you of. Put on a three-yard trace of not *too* fine gut, for the barbel is a big fish. A float? Yes, certainly a float. I use one of the little red pilots of the pike tackle, but any float will do provided it is not *too* corpulent. To the end of the trace attach a single bait hook and such weight (here the envelope leads are in their element) as the water to be fished calls for. But the minnow must be fished fairly deep. Pass the hook through the bait's upper lip and swim it down any, not too heavy, stream, or mill-tail, that you suspect of fish. Be careful to keep a straight line and thus avoid the float reaching the shoal before the bait. I do not think that this question of precedence is an over-alarming one, but it is well to take no risks, and nothing is so slovenly to see as the float-first, Jack before his master, all anyhow style of angling.

Instead of a large minnow, or a small gudgeon, you may fish, by this method, with cheese-paste or gentles, two or three threaded on to the hook, or indeed with any of the usual Thames variants. Oh yes, and if your minnows are all little minnows it is well to use a small triangle instead of the single hook. And to each hook of the triangle a minnow. This rule of three is often extremely successful. If a barbel responds to it, he will take with a nibble, a suck and a little pull. Give him a half-foot of line before you hit him. But if it is trout that comes, he will probably have you with a tear and a bang and be fifty yards from the punt's till or ever you, white-faced with excitement, are on to your feet.

Thus barbel may be taken with live-bait which is no natural food of theirs. Though, of a dark, blue summer night, and the moon in it as golden as an apricot, you may see a big barbel gourmet come up along the camp sheathing after the minnow shoals. He does not splash and dash among them as do the predatory fishes. But the minnows, to see him, crowd all against the sheathing in a cloud. And the barbel, coming close, opens his mouth and seems to suck into it a tithe of the school. He seems to inhale minnows rather than catch them. And then he lounges upon his way. But you will linger for a minute and listen to the nightingale that sings in the vicarage garden.

And that reminds me that a barbel can sing too. I think he is the only fish that can. On such a summer night as that on which he went minnowing just now you may hear him sing. In the quiet comes a croaking, then a chorus of small, snoring, puffing grunts. These noises are the barbel singing on the moonlit shallows because of their summer *joie de vivre*. They raise their blunt and bearded noses to the surface and above it. And I suppose that the sound they make is caused by some outblowing of air. But, like the nightingale's, it is a song of summer and the velvet dark.

A big barbel was the subject of a 'fisherman's lie' story of which I saw the finish. There came a young soldier to the middle Thames in May. He thought that he would catch a trout or two by spinning, a method in which he excelled. But he was infirm of purpose and faint in pursuit. Soon he was finding base recreation in foul-hooking the barbel upon the shallow below the weir. He, of course, returned to the water, most lovingly, any that he landed.

Presently he pulled his blue phantom into a great golden-brown back. His rod was a very small and light rod, his tackle was the most gossamer that credit could procure. He was a good fisherman, but in about twenty minutes the barbel broke him and won free.

The gut had smashed at the swivel ring on the phantom's nose. But some days later the angler was at it again with a new phantom. The Thames is a big river and the barbel in him are many. So it was a wonderful thing that the fisherman should again fall foul of his fish of last Friday. Yet this is just what he did do. And this time he landed the barbel. In fact I netted the fish for him. He was a great lump of a fish and we weighed him before we put him back. He went eleven pounds and some ounces. But the real miracle was that a single hook of the new minnow's triangle had passed through the ring of the swivel of the minnow already in the barbel's back. And without other hold than that the fish was caught and the earlier gear recovered.

If ever you want to ascertain the weight of a fish before restoring it to the river the simplest and safest way is thus. In most fishing punts there is a towel. Lay the fish in it, knot the towel by the four corners and suspend upon the scale. Knock an ounce or so off the result and the nett weight will be that of the fish, who may now be returned to the river with thanks and compliments.

You may also take barbel with the little spinning-rod, the one with the china rings. No float is here required. Only a sea-trout trace, with swivels, and just enough lead pinched on to it to carry out a fair length of undressed line. Attach a Stewart tackle to the gut. Procure a dozen or so brandling worms in moss and a mustard tin. You say that the brightness of the stream behind the mill is, this June evening, brown cloudy with the shapes of barbel? Very well.

Row the punt to the tail of the run and anchor her to rock gently out of the current. Put on a brandling and cast it upstream upon a long line to dribble back to you, you winding, slowly, in along the bed of the river, among the big brown shadows. Presently you will get, I hope you will get, a quiet little pull, which, upon the strike will develop into the heavy tug of a hooked fish. But before you go to this form of fishing, or any other form of barbel fishing, be sure that you know first where the fish are, for where there are no barbel there will be no sport with them.

I have kept the jolliest way of barbelling for the last. Here is no leger with its lead that is always catching up on the bottom and wanting 'hands' and patience to coax it forth from the weeds that it lurks among. Here no lobs, lively or languid, are a necessity. Here are no anæmic gentles to manhandle. Nor pastes to manipulate nor living minnow to make, possibly, uncomfortable.

Take the live-bait rod then, the light, old split-cane. No float is necessary above the three yards of gut to which a small lead or so may be attached. Your hook must be a small triangle. This warm August evening the barbel are in the shrunken weir pool. The water that trickles over the moss-grown steps and falls tinkling among the piles is clear and warm. The silkweed is up and the barbel have been feeding on it for the last few sunny days. But I do not think that they eat the weed *qua* weed. They eat it because it is the overcrowded home, just now, of the water shrimp or snail after his myriad kind. But for whatever reason they eat it, eat it they do, browsing along the sill like a row of brown cows in a byre.

In this clear water the barbel is shy, far shyer than a girl. So creep most cautiously and slink like a shadow until you get to where such stream that remains will carry your light tackle down upon it. There now, you say, the bait has been forgotten? Jump to no conclusions, my son. Rather, stand very, very still; so still that in our suits of sober grey flannel we may be taken for part of the Conservancy's grey painted posts and railings.

The Protean herds are still browsing. So, quietly, drop the bare triangle into that straggle of bright silk-weed. And quietly lift it out again. You see that the hook has baited itself? The little green streamer that now hangs drippingly upon it is lure enough. So float it quietly down upon the lazy current and the first eleven-pounder that it meets with will, I hope, gently inhale it. And then I can assure you that the fun will be furious and prolonged. And when it is over we will steal along, a-tiptoe, to a fresh coign, re-bait the triangle and try again.

And know this. The barbel when caught is a fine meaty fellow and makes, as I hope I may show you later, an excellent kettle of fish. But, and better even than this excellent quality, he is the most stubborn fighter that swims in Thames water and, in cunning and caprice, foxes and Christmas cock pheasants are fools to him. The man who goes out to catch our Thames barbel and comes home with a one or a two after each outing may indeed call himself a fisherman and hold his head high in the Houghton Club or in the tap-room of 'The Perch and Pike'.

But best of all I love the barbels because they roll like big, brown-and-white cats upon golden shallows and sing in the moonlight with the *joie de vivre* of June. And because, so, they are all Thames to me and wild-rose time and the streams running down from the weir.

## The Barbel Swim

*Peter Wheat*

Let us now discuss an average barbel swim. The river will be flowing along at a fair pace over a bed of gravel and silt deposits. Weeds will be growing in clumps dotted along the bottom, with the green fronds trailing downstream to form long narrow channels. During the day barbel lie under these weed-beds where you can see their tails exposed as the fronds waver in the current. Occasionally they will follow particles of food downstream. During the summer months this is the normal daytime activity of barbel. It might be thought that they remain in the same area during the daylight hours, but in fact this is not so, and they spend a considerable amount of time patrolling along the same route. Often I have seen shoals of barbel moving upstream or dropping downstream. During the day they pass close to the bank in certain spots at regular intervals. This movement has been made extremely clear to me while fishing the Dorset Stour. In one swim they enter at the downstream end and pass up through close to the bank. In clear conditions they can be further observed from a tree as they drop back down the centre of the river before again entering the swim downstream to repeat a cycle which, provided there is no disturbance, lasts throughout the day. It is clear that this is the same shoal, because for no apparent reason a tench around the four pound mark tags along with them, often, in fact, leading the shoal!

This is just one water, but I think it is safe to say that this is the normal habit of barbel in all waters. I remember one classic example of this patrolling habit bringing success to an angler in difficult conditions. The scene was the very famous Railway Pool on the Royalty Fisheries during an exceptionally dry summer, when the river was abnormally low. In fact there were only a few feet of water in the pool, which is one of the deepest in the fishery. Conditions for fishing of any sort were almost impossible, and very little had been caught for some time. The angler in question had been watching a small shoal of big barbel cruising slowly in the clear water and it was not long before a pattern emerged which brought the fish past the same points each time. By carefully lowering a piece of cheese to the nearest of these points he was able to hook three fish before the shoal were scared off. The fish weighed over 10 lb each. A red letter catch, and even more so with conditions against taking a single fish.

The average barbel swim is best legered downstream. After baiting up, the cast is made downstream and across, a little way past the centre of the stream. A small amount of line is allowed to come from the spool before the bale arm is brought into position and the line tightened up. At first the leger weight will move with the pressure of the current until it settles into position. Some anglers use a rest for this sort of fishing, but few bother to position it correctly. When I am holding the rod I usually sit facing downstream with the rod held high in order to keep as much line out of the water as possible, to help in detecting fine bites and to aid a clean strike. If I use a rest, which is rare in this fishing, it is because the bites are few and far between. I position it so that the rod is angled into the air in much the same way as when I am holding it.

The typical barbel bite which slams the rod-top over is the exception rather than the rule. It is more often a case of slight touches or tremors. These sort of bites vary so much that the best advice is to strike at anything which feels unusual. Bites are sometimes hard to interpret from the knocks and touches caused by the current, but I have found in my fishing that false bites register on the rod-top, while those caused by the fish are felt through the line as well. Perhaps the most common barbel bite of all is a couple of slight knocks followed by the rod bending slowly over, and it is rare to miss such an indication. Another type of bite, which is not hard to hit, feels like a saw being drawn across the line. This is caused by the barbel holding the bait but not moving off. It is a slight but positive indication which should be struck immediately.

There has been considerable difference of opinion concerning the length of trail between hook and leger weight. Some prefer long trails of three feet or more, while others consider short trails of 12 inches are better. The real answer is that both long and short trails are suitable at the right time in the right swim. Non-buoyant baits like cheese, sausage, or worm, are best fished on a long trail in weedy swims, whilst other baits, like crust, which has a tendency to rise in the water, obviously require a very short trail of a few inches or less. A short trail is also useful if the bites are weak or tentative.

When a barbel is hooked among the weeds there is absolutely no need to panic. The desire to wind it in before snagging occurs is the easiest way to lose the fish. If you wind the fish upstream it certainly will snag you, but provided a steady pressure is kept up without winding, the fish will try to get away downstream. Work your way down the bank until you are below the fish, from which position you can apply pressure which sends the fish boring upstream and under the weeds. Keep up a steady pressure until its strength ebbs, and you can work it little by little to the waiting net. Sometimes, if the barbel is a very big one, this may take as long as 10 or 15 minutes. Never be in too much of a hurry to land a barbel. Quite often it is impatience which loses the fish. Even though it may be close under your feet it is very likely to make one or two further runs, so be prepared to slacken off when it does.

Over the last few years there has been much discussion in the angling Press regarding the fighting merits of barbel in various waters. One side maintain that barbel in some waters are powerful fish which make long runs, while those in other waters have little fight because the tussle is nothing less than a tug-of-war. I think the fighting merits of barbel should be judged by the water they come from. In the Thames, for instance, they do give long, hard, powerful runs in an effort to find cover, while in the Avon a barbel makes a short run and is immediately under a weed-bed - which to any fish is safety enough and it does not have a desire to go rushing off elsewhere. Obviously the fight could be called a tug-of-war, but is a hard, dogged game where there is just as much fighting strength as you get from a barbel which runs. Even in weedy waters, barbel do make runs when there are suitable snags in the vicinity. In the Royalty, barbel make repeated attempts to double back round salmon stones, and at such times they really move. During the summer of 1965 I fished a weedy swim in the Railway Pool. The fish I caught were all hooked in a small slack at the tail of a large weed-bed. Most of them burrowed under the weeds at first, before coming out to make long determined runs towards a salmon stone on the far side. Either the barbel got round the stone, or, more likely, a break occurred while trying to hold the hooked fish.

Some swims are better fished by legering upstream from the tail of the swim. Whenever possible I prefer this method, which leaves you in an excellent playing position from the time the fish is hooked. It is important that the lead is just sufficient to hold bottom and no more - heavy leads defeat the whole object behind this upstream legering. After making the cast upstream and across, the line is made as tight as possible without dislodging the tackle. A rest can be used, but it is far better to hold the rod high with as much line out of the water as possible. Bites will mainly be indicated by the line falling slack on the surface as the leger is dislodged. This could be caused by the action of the current but the slight difference between the two can be detected with experience. The differences are, however, slight, and I would rather strike every time the line goes slack than miss a chance. To strike a slack line bite, the rod-top is quickly lowered while you wind furiously to take up slack, making a strike over the shoulder at the same time. The fish, if hooked, is played from the downstream position.

Apart from legering in these static ways, a leger can be used to search an area very effectively if it is made to roll. Very little weight is used for the rolling leger method, whilst baits which cover the hook are to be preferred to the ones which leave the point exposed. By casting straight out from the bank and letting the bait trundle round, you can cover an arc of water which is further increased as each cast is made, until the far bank is reached. Future casts are made to the far bank but each time slightly downstream. A great deal of water can be searched in this way, and a rolling bait is quite often preferred to a static one on hot summer days. Provided the correct amount of lead is used, relative to the speed of the current, any hold-ups can be dealt with by a slight lift of the rod-top to start the bait rolling again. Bites are usually very definite, jagging knocks which are very easy to connect with.

Apart from the normal barbel swims which have at least a little flow, barbel in two waters I know have a fondness for feeding in slackwater swims - mainly during the evening. This occurs in waters which are fished by a large number of anglers where groundbait, maggots, etc. are brought downstream by the current to collect in the slacks just off the main flow. Barbel recognise such places as feeding spots - whilst they prefer faster water, they are quite prepared to move in during the evening and night to scavenge for food. Many of these slacks are little more than a few feet out from the bank, which makes them ideal for ultra light legering. During the afternoon the swim is well baited up in readiness for the evening, when the sun has left the water and the barbel begin to feed. Provided you are reasonably quiet, it is possible to take quite a few barbel in a very short while. Again you can use a rest, although it is probably better to hold the rod, bearing in mind that you can expect quite a few bites while the fish are feeding in the swim. A purely personal preference on my part is to use a centre-pin reel for this close-in fishing.

Night fishing for barbel can be great fun where it is

allowed, although my biggest regret is not being able to practise it on the Avon and Stour, where I am convinced some tremendous fish could be taken. Nights which are still and humid, with no moon to brighten the scene are the best. Always get to know the river and the barbel-holding swims during the daylight hours, before any attempt is made to fish them at night. When the ability to see what you are doing has gone, the information gained during the daylight hours is invaluable. I like to get in the swim, tackled-up, and the groundbaiting done long before darkness falls. All the things I might need during the night are laid out on a piece of rubber sheet, so that I know where they are when I need them without rummaging through my bag. The less you use a torch the better, but if you have one on during the night to change tackle, make sure it has a red face and keep it off the water as much as possible. By all means shine a beam on the water when a good fish is being landed - it is far better to be sure, than lose a big one through being 'too pukka'.

Waters like the Lower Thames fish far better for barbel during the dark hours, when the disturbance from river traffic is at a minimum, and I know some stretches of the Kennet where barbel are never caught before dusk. The same, I understand, applies to Severn fish. Methods for night fishing are exactly the same as for legering during the day, although I feel that a static leger downstream is the most satisfactory of all, with less chance of getting hung up or mis-casting. Night fishing for barbel can be very effective on waters over-run with anglers during the day. It is a great pity that a lot of good barbel-holding waters also have bans on night fishing. Some of these are warranted, whilst others could easily be lifted to give keen anglers a little more scope for fishing.

In winter the small amount of barbel fishing I do is with a light leger in the slacks which form after the winter floods.

Altogether legering is an interesting and enjoyable method of fishing, which is not very hard to learn once the 'chuck-it-and-chance-it' idea has been dispelled. Used correctly it is a highly successful way to take barbel in all waters.

## The Barbel and How to Bait for Him

*Philip Geen*

Shall I write of the upper reaches or the lower? Shall we go up from Old Windsor towards the river's rise or down from Egham Lock towards its fall, down past Staines, The Hook, Laleham, Chertsey Weir and bridge, past Dumsey Deeps? - Stay a moment here; it was Dumsey Deeps I baited for the best friend Thames fish ever had.

He was also the kindest possible patron to the professional fishermen, yet not one amongst their number, try how they would, and no doubt they tried their best, could ever show him sport.

For some years I resided quite near this spot and I offered him a bed and a try with me. He accepted an invitation for that day week and, in the meantime, I baited three barbel swims; Dumsey Deeps was one. I longed to give him sport and, to ensure success, I baited each swim night and morning with ever-increasing doses of well-scoured lobs.

Life comes to food in growing numbers; feed your sparrows for a week and see.

In a dark cool outhouse I kept four tubs - casks cut in halves - well supplied with moss. Little village folks brought tins, jugs and utensils various filled with worms captured by candle-light the night before and these were stock for tub No. 1, to be promoted, when searched over, to No. 2 and so on until they reached No. 4, by which time they were red, tough and so inviting that sport would surely attend the using of them.

The little army of wormers soon grew numerous as, in addition to their pay of sixpence per quart, they often got pats and smiles and a lump of cake.

Barbel like to grub for food in deep holes that have rugged hard bottoms in, or near, the strongest and heaviest stream. If the stream is very strong I use clay so as to sink the worms quickly. It is at the very commencement of the hole you must draw your fish when ledger fishing, which is the method most likely to get the largest. I make the clay into dumplings, with worms inside them, and drop them so that they may sink to the spot where the baited hook will go.

I much prefer the ledger to a float as with the latter there is sure to come a desire to go the full length of the hole and then give a swishing strike that is very like to spoil the chances.

When these fish are on the feed they come in turn to the clay balls, grub out a worm, put their side across the stream and are away to the rear of all the shoal, where they again wait their turn. Sometimes they come in double file, but always in drill-like order, and therefore care is needed not to be too quick in striking at them or you may prick a fish that will leave the hole and take all the others with him. The preliminary nibble means only 'now look out', so wait for the drawing pull, and, when that comes, strike quickly and hold as firmly, just for a moment, as the fine tackle you should use for barbel justifies.

It was a useful nine foot rod that I lent my guest. It tapered so that the finest gut could bend it almost double, and yet it never wobbled, and the spring that was in the top helped the wielder of it to cast the smallest bullet. My finest dark-dyed, silk plaited line was used, and to it was joined a yard of stained gut, at the finer end of which was a No. 6 hook. A bullet just sufficient for its purpose was selected, and was kept from sliding towards the hook by a split shot, nipped on the gut thirty inches from it.

You can fancy how carefully I chose two maiden lobs and how particular I was to put them on the hook so that their heads and tails could wag enticingly.

My anxiety was great that morning and I would willingly have bartered a lengthened period of lucky fishing to ensure success that day.

Fortune favoured me; the flood that had been running cleared from day to day and, on the morning of our start, the water was just perfection, a little cloudy. The sky had ever-shifting driving clouds which hid the sun, and the up-stream wind gave a lovely ripple that aided the dark water to hide our movements in the punt. Through the full leaved branches of the withy boughs the breeze came with hiss and whisper to fan our cheeks and help to make us hopeful. Would the promise thus held out be fulfilled?

I asked to be allowed to make the first cast for him, and, as I handed back the rod, he looked at me, saw what was in my mind, and laughingly warned me that he was the most awful Jonah that ever held a rod.

For quite five minutes the punt seemed to me to be full, from head to tail, of breathing expectancy, and then followed fears of failure. I thought back to discover a mistake. Had I overbaited, or baited so late that the eels had got the worms? Should I up poles and on to the next swim? At last I thought of a plan it is always well to try. I scattered a little food. I threw in half a dozen broken worms well up stream so that they might sink towards the fish which might be merely hanging back, waiting for the feeding-time they had grown to expect. It answered. At last I saw the top jig, jig, and then the whole rod bend as the fish attempted his journey to the rear.

For full two hours the fish kept the fisher and his assistant busy, and, when the lull came (it only lasted a few minutes) I availed myself of it to give them more dumplings with just a broken worm or two at which they could come and nozzle but not fill themselves.

By lunch-time the fish were packed in the bottom of the well as sheep are in a pen so, to make room for others, I, in obedience to the orders of my guest, put all the fish, excepting only two, back into the river. It need scarcely be said I took them far enough down stream to ensure they would tell no tales of those we still desired to catch.

The afternoon's fishing was without a break in its success. The luncheon hour's rest and the provoking clay balls had evidently made the fish hungrily anxious for the luscious worms that had accompanied the clay on previous days. No sooner had the baited hook found its resting-place than it was seized and the rod was bent with the efforts of a fish to go rearwards.

It was a wonderful day and a wondrous take of barbel for one man to get.

So the promise of the morning was gloriously fulfilled. I have a rod to commemorate that day, much too grand for use, which has inscribed upon its butt 'From Thomas Spreckley to Philip Geen'. Yes, my guest was the late Thomas Spreckley, so long the president of the T.A.P.S.

I am pleased to write these few words, in my poor book, of his work for anglers. I am thinking, and it's so, no doubt, that the good he did by his deeds of charity to needy folk is written of elsewhere.

* * *

Alongside is the splendid trout-shallow known to all Thames fishermen. One day I saw three good fish feeding here at one and the same time and, for a moment, we hoped that our bait would have been seized. Several times they fed but each time it travelled over them, with the usual result.

Up with the weight, let the punt drift with the rapid stream, and, as she goes, we may feel thankful that our evening's meal does not depend on a trout, to catch which may take you longer than it shall to get seven years older.

As we round the bend there are some excellent swims where the bank angler may come. I should bring an extra rod and use it with a ledger. Let it be a two ounce flat lead that it may have a chance of remaining where you throw it, but there should be at least one yard of gut between this formidable piece of metal and the worm.

Try between the withy trees, slyly if the water is low and clear, but, should you be fortunate enough to find it high and a little coloured, you may stand boldly forward. Your take will only be limited by the time and skill devoted to its capture; to the bank the fish must come for rest and food while such a water is running.

The last tree hangs more out over the river than the rest, and under it is the noted barbel swim, to fish which I have pushed my punt oftener than I can ever hope to do again.

Locally this hole is known and spoken of as Colnbrook Churchyard. During the time I resided at Wraysbury I made several attempts to discover why it had been so named, but I could never get beyond the general belief that the Hounslow Heath highwaymen, who frequently made Colnbrook their headquarters, used to sink their victims in this deep hole.

The last time I came here I was early, yet too late. As we rounded the corner we saw that it was already occupied by a punt, in which there was a gentleman, a lady, and a boy, and as we were deciding what we were to do, I saw the gentleman strike a fish, and then ensued one of the grandest struggles I had seen for many a long day.

Everything favoured the fish - a heavy stream was running, and if, with the aid of this he could only get fifteen short yards down stream, he would have no difficulty in regaining his liberty. There, in the deep hole, lies a tree, branches and all, as washed from a spot 500 yards up-stream, where it toppled into the river. Many a good fish that could, and ought to have been prevented, has done this little rush clean off the reel, much to the astonishment of sundry fishers who were not too clever by half at barbel fishing.

Today the battle is pretty equal. A score of times, at least, the fish came within a yard or two of home, to be got back to the punt bit by bit, and, when he could no longer keep the bottom, he rolled over and over on the surface in such a manner as would have broken any tackle had not line been given. Back it was coaxed again, and, had I been in the punt, it would have been near enough to have reached it with the net. The lady made an attempt, but it was too far off.

The next time it came back she made another try, and failed. The gentleman said something which I fancied caused her to lose confidence, and, instead of keeping her net a little under water for the fish to come into it, she was holding it ready to drop when told. The gentleman gave the word; but, instead of putting it under, she, with exhausted nerve, dropped it on the fish, and so ended the struggle between Mr, Mrs and Master Phillips and a twelve pound barbel.

## No Need to Lie

*Dick Walker*

The biggest barbel I ever caught came from the Hampshire Avon, but not from Christchurch. Avon barbel originally entered the river from its joint estuary with the Stour; they were put into the latter river, but some decided they liked the Avon better. They've been working upstream since, and now the biggest fish are to be found in the middle reaches of the river. I say they are to be found; in fact they take a lot of finding, and they aren't easily caught when found. This I discovered when I went to fish at Ibsley, with Peter Thomas.

We had made arrangements with Col. S. H. Crow, who looks after the Ibsley fishing, for some ground-baiting to be done before we came. Col. Crow is a really great character - a fine salmon angler who takes a keen interest in coarse-fishing. He pulls our legs unmercifully, pretending to despise coarse-fishing, and every time we go to Ibsley and hunt along the river bank for him, we find him sitting on a stool, coarse-fishing! He put in the chopped cheese groundbait for a week; then Peter and I arrived to fish.

We found the groundbaiting had been most successful - the chosen swim must have been paved with eels. The large quantities of medium-sized chub that had also moved into it must have been brave, with all those eels about! If any barbel were in the swim, it was clear that the chub and the eels would always beat them to the bait; so after a couple of days Pete and I decided to try elsewhere.

Pete caught several 4 lb chub and one 5-pounder. I kept searching for barbel. In the afternoon of our third day, when Col. Crow, Pete and I were prospecting along the banks, I found one. It wasn't easy to see. At first I wasn't sure whether it was a fish or a streamer of brown weed; the current was curling the surface. But as I stared, I began to make out the pink ventral fins and then the big pectorals, like the ears of an African elephant. Pete and Col. Crow came and stared too, and after a while they also got it clearly in focus. We agreed it was a big fish, and thought it might go as much as 14 lb. After a few minutes one of us must have moved quickly; the barbel shot off in the cloud of disturbed sand.

I marked the spot carefully, and that evening I returned to it with a Chapman MK IV carp rod, and Intrepid reel holding 200 yards of 11 lb nylon line and my big carp landing net. On the line was a 1 oz Arlesey bomb and a number 1 gilt incurved hook, baited with three big lobworms. The patch of yellow gravel where the barbel had been was easy to find; it was no more than 7 or 8 feet from the bank, and I lowered the baited hook to rest exactly in the middle of it. Then I moved 20 yards upstream, paying out line. I put the rod in a rest, made myself comfortable and settled down to wait.

It was a fine, warm evening and very pleasant to sit beside such a beautiful lively river. I saw a small animal jumping about on the opposite bank which I couldn't identify at first; then I realised it was a mink and remembered Col. Crow had said that these animals, escapees from mink farms, were becoming quite common in Hampshire. They were very destructive of game and smaller birds, and he had shot several of them.

Presently some very big chub began to move in the slack water across the river and I was tempted to wind in and cast across to them. There was really no certainty that the barbel we had seen would return to the same spot. I couldn't even feel that this was likely; barbel do not occupy an exact spot as do trout. Then

I thought I had better stick it out; I'd come to Ibsley to fish for barbel, and it would be silly to use the time fishing for chub, which I could catch nearer home.

I was glad I didn't wind in, for just after it had become too dark to see the line, the rod-top jerked and then went down with a bang. If I hadn't grabbed the butt, it would have gone into the river. There was no need to strike; the fish had hooked itself, and was going away downstream with such power and speed that I thought it must be a salmon.

A willow tree prevented me following it for more than about 20 yards; there I had to stop. I increased the pressure on the fish, and it slowed down, then ran across the river into the slack water on the far side. I could see tremendous swirls as it plunged about, apparently trying to get into the forest of rushes; but I had strong tackle and bore on it for all I was worth. It worked upstream on the far side; then came across, under the rod-point, and made a powerful rush upstream into the fast water that was thick with great beds and streamers of ranunculus. There it dug itself into the weeds. I knew now it must be a barbel, and that provided I didn't do anything silly I would get it out of these weeds. I did, too - several times, and then back it would go. But eventually, it tired, and I had it under control.

By now it was really dark. I had moved back almost

to where I had been sitting when I hooked the fish, so it wasn't difficult to get my torch out of the bag. What was difficult was to hold a torch, a rod and a landing net with only two hands, especially as the current was very strong. As soon as the big carp net was dipped in the water, this strong current nearly tore it from my hand. I must have made five or six attempts to net that fish, with the torch jammed between my knees, the rod in my right hand and the net in my left. Each time I missed the fish, the current swept it 10 or 12 yards downstream and I had to take the net from the water, lay it down and pump the fish back again.

At last, with the fish quite inert and at the surface, I dropped the rod, took both hands to the net and by good luck got the fish in the mesh. Out it came, and out came the spring balance. 12 3/4 lb it weighed, a very fine barbel and the best I have ever taken. But it was very whacked. I knew I should have to put it back at once if it were to survive.

So I took the hook out, knelt down on the bank and held my barbel on an even keel till he recovered his strength. It took a long time, and I began to wonder whether he had taken too much. But he began to move from side to side, and then suddenly shot away with a great splash that sent water in my face and down my neck. I was glad.

I've been back to look at that patch of gravel several times, hoping to see my barbel on it, with perhaps a couple of pounds of weight added. He's never been there.

### *Kennet Barbel*

Like many other anglers, I have caught plenty of barbel in the lower reaches of the Avon, including several big ones up to 12 1/2 lb; but in the confined area of the river there, and with bankside crowds, and litter strewn everywhere, I have never greatly enjoyed the fishing. With the barbel in the adjacent river Stour, I confess I have so far failed almost completely, the biggest barbel I have taken so far from that river weighing only a little over 6 lb.

For sport rather than sheer size, the barbel in the Thames and the Kennet are supreme. I like the Kennet best because the country through which it runs is, for the most part, prettier. Although Kennet barbel sometimes reach great size, most of the shoals are of fish between 3 and 5 lb, and it is quite common to catch half a dozen of them in an afternoon's fishing. On suitable light tackle they fight like wild-cats, and when you hook an extra-big one and land it, you feel you've deserved it.

The biggest Kennet barbel I've ever caught weighed 7 lb, and on a 3 lb line and number 10 hook it took ten minutes to land, a wonderful fighter. Catching that one was really responsible for my losing the biggest barbel I've ever hooked, because it encouraged me in the notion that light tackle is the stuff to use for Kennet barbel-fishing.

It certainly produces more bites, and you get more sport with the average shoal fish, but if you hook one of the rare monsters, you will be depending much more on luck than on skill in dealing with it.

A week after catching my 7-pounder, I hooked an enormous barbel on my little rod and fine line. It tore 50 yards upstream, close to the opposite bank, with me running after it full pelt. Then it turned, crossed the river and came down in the fast water on my side. I never expected to land it but I thought if I gave it all the stick the tackle would stand, I might get a look at what I was sure to lose. In that I succeeded.

I got that barbel to the surface twice. It was huge. If I'd had a friend with a big, long-handled net nearby, the fish might possibly have been landed, but I was on a bank 5 feet above the water-level and my net was only 18 inches across. The barbel was twice as long as that, at least, and it was in a quick current.

I went downstream with it until I came to an

overhanging willow that I couldn't pass. There I opened the reel pickup, pulled off all the line remaining on the spool, tied the end to a twig and rushed round the willow. I fished up the line, pulled in the end, which I had to break off somewhere between me and the twig, threaded it feverishly through the rod rings and just got it tied to the spool again as it came taut. It tightened up, quite slowly, to a twangy state, then there came a heavy tug, and all went slack. I reeled up to find the lead still there but the hook gone.

I felt none of the helplessness and disappointment that losing a monster fish usually causes, because I'd never felt the slightest hope of landing that barbel; but I use heavier tackle and carry a more suitable net when barbel-fishing in the Kennet now. I might hook the same one again!

## The Tiger of the Weir Pool

*Colin Willock*

We were well into September now, and still I hadn't taken Bob fishing for barbel. When autumn fades, the barbel fade with it and disappear into the deep holes of the river bed to weather out the winter. So we hadn't got much time left. I had purposely delayed our expedition until Bob had had a fair amount of practice with the more docile breeds, for the barbel is a tiger-fish. He is tough, leather-mouthed, and quite as strong as the salmon.

Where would you expect to find him, then? Certainly not in any meandering backwater or quiet eddy. The barbel is a tough customer who likes to live hard and rough. His haunts are found, as you might have guessed, where the current is strongest and the pools deepest, where the water tumbles over the weir-lasher, scooping out a deep, troubled pit from the river bed. These are the places where you must look for the fighting barbel.

Naturally, there aren't many rivers in England which can provide sufficient stream to suit his lordship. The Hampshire Avon, that king of all coarse-fishing rivers, is one; so is the Trent; so too, is the mighty Thames. Many London fishermen, therefore, know the thrill of angling for the gamest of them all.

There is only one snag to the whole exciting business of barbel-fishing - considerable previous ground-baiting is necessary. I don't say you *won't* catch barbel if you don't haunt your swim for days beforehand, bearing sacks of garden worms. I know men who live near Shepperton Lock on the Thames who come down from their riverside houses nightly and, without any preliminary skirmishing, generally hook a good barbel from the gravelly run below the weir. All I do know is that your chances of connecting with this fish are much more certain if you *can* introduce some propaganda into the pool before you begin.

In the old days, fishermen used to think nothing of tossing in a thousand or more lobs. But nowadays we have neither the time nor the money for such extravagancies; and, to tell the truth, history doesn't relate whether the old masters caught any more fish than we do!

One thing only does the barbel have in common with the sluggish bream for which we last fished:

you can't get up too early or go out too late in the evening to catch him.

Bob and I were down at the Thames weir which we had chosen for our attack upon the barbel at 6 am, and, believe me, it can be quite chilly at that hour on a September morning!

We shivered as we loaded our tackle into the punt which we had hired from the lock-keeper for the morning's sport; and there was that gentleman himself to see us on our way.

I had met the lock-keeper on previous expeditions, and I knew that his method of ground-baiting was a good one.

The evening before we had rowed over the weir pool dropping quantities of lobworms into the eddy in such a way that they would be taken round and round until they had settled on the bottom where the barbel lay. To do this, very nice calculation of the course of the eddy was necessary. Otherwise the worms would have been caught in the main current and washed away.

## *Two Men in a Boat*

Bob was so keen to get off that he was all for piling into the punt and putting up his rod once we were on the water. There are several excellent reasons why I persuaded Bob to be more patient and to tackle up on dry land.

For one thing, you've no idea until you've tried it what a tangle two men assembling rods in a small boat can get into. Second, one or both of the men may fall in. And last, but certainly not least, the less noise you make in a boat, the better. The bang of a heavy boot on the bottom-boards or the clang of a bait-can falling into the well of the punt sounds like a thunderclap to the waiting barbel, who, I am certain, always keep their 'ears' laid well back and ready for trouble.

We sat ourselves in our fishing stations in the boat, laid out our tackle neatly, settled down comfortably, and, with a hefty shove from the lock-keeper, who probably soundly cursed us for getting him out of bed, headed out towards the weir.

It is a grand but rather frightening feeling fishing below a large weir-lashing. The water crashes down and sweeps past in a way that threatens to take you away with it. Actually, you're quite safe so long as you don't go nearer than two boat's lengths of the fall. Anyway, we were heading for the calm eddy at the left side of the lasher, where a large wooden post stood out of the water. An early-morning mist rose off the crest of the fall, so that the water appeared to be smoking.

We tied up our bows to the post, then allowed the stern to swing until the punt was pointing down the pool. I now lowered the punt pole quietly over the stern and, having forced it into the bottom, lashed us firmly to it.

When fishing from a boat, remember you must secure *both* ends or else you will swing, and your tackle will be dragged all over the bottom.

We were now ready to bait up. Worms, gentles, and, early in the season, caddis grubs are the finest bait for barbel. But worms are the best stand-by. The great thing to remember is that, whatever bait you use, *it must be fished on the bottom*.

Bob asked the depth of water and I told him 14 feet. His face dropped. His rod was only 12 feet long, so how could he get our 14 feet or more of line and still cast? It seemed as though for once Bob was going to have to give up his favourite float-fishing. He looked crestfallen when I suggested that he ledger, even when I explained that this method usually takes the best barbel. So I took pity on him and admitted that there *was* a way out.

I now produced from my tackle box a sliding float for use in deep water. It was the first time Bob had heard of such a thing, so perhaps I had better describe it.

The only real difference between a slider and any other float is that it has no cap to hold the line fast.

Instead, there is a wire loop at the top of it, just as there is at the bottom. The line passes through both these, leaving the float free to slide up and down.

When you cast, the float rests on your top shot. As it hits the water, the line sinks through the wire loops to the bottom. Finally, the weight of the line on the bottom loop pulls the float into the cocked position.

This all sounds too good to be true, you may say. It is! For one thing, the sliding float is not so sensitive as one that is fixed to the line (though there is a way of getting round this). What is more, given the slightest current, the wretched thing twists and turns itself round the line in a desperate manner which makes you wish you had never bothered with it.

However, here the water was fairly still, so I told Bob it would probably work all right. Oh yes! I said there was a way of making the contraption sensitive to bites. There is, though it requires very careful plumbing of depth. Once you have found exactly where the top of the sliding float meets the line, reel in and tie a piece of rubber band to the line at that point. Cut off the loose ends, leaving a knot of rubber small enough to pass through your rod rings when casting. Now cast afresh, and the best of luck! If all goes well, the line flies out, the bait sinks, the rubber knot comes to rest against the top loop of your float. All you have to do now is to get a bite, and the rubber will act as a stop and pull the float under. I *have* known it work, but for me it's the ledger every time. Anyway, after only a bit of fiddling, Bob got his line out and his sliding float was sitting pretty.

## *Fighting Fish*

Meantime, I threw out a ledger near to the edge of the fast water. In these conditions a round bullet may get swept down the stream-bed, so I was using a flat lead shaped like a box and known as a 'coffin lead'. The idea of this is that it will not roll over and over on the bottom in the current. The coffin lead is bored down the centre, of course, to allow the wire or gut to pass through it.

We were fishing at last! With barbel you cannot afford to put the rod down and forget it, for the big ones often bite the most shyly. I rested my rod on the side of the boat and let the line run over the back of my fingers. In this way I could feel the slightest nibble from the fish. I was ready to respond with an instant but not too violent strike.

I hadn't long to wait. The bite which I felt was certainly no nibble. It was a solid thump such as these fish sometimes give.

I struck, and held the fish as hard as my 2x gut and 6 lb line would allow, to get the hook - a No. 6 with the worm threaded on to it - home into his armoured mouth.

Then the fish began his barbelish tricks. From where I sat it felt as though he was standing on his head and trying to bury himself deep into the gravel in an attempt to cut the line. Then he would be up in mid-water, rolling to dive again, letting me get a little line back only to rip it off the reel once more. Once he went to the bottom and I thought I had lost him round an under-water obstruction. I put on all the pressure I dared and still couldn't budge him. I was just beginning to curse my bad luck when the line gave the slightest tremor. He was still there! He had probably flicked his tail in annoyance.

When a heavy fish goes to ground, I have found there is only one thing to do. I daren't skull-haul this one, because I guessed he was somewhere near the maximum weight of my line - and the strength of a 6 lb line is much less when the line is wet and knotted. So I broke all fishing rules and let the fish have a slack line.

For a few seconds there was no answer. Then, feeling he was free, the barbel ceased to sulk and made off once more. The check on my reel stopped his first rush, so he was evidently tiring now. After two more little dashes, we had him alongside the punt - a fine 6-pounder if ever I saw one. We weighed him, and I pointed out the four barbules at his mouth which I had remarked upon when gudgeon fishing. We looked at his olive-green back, shading to golden brown on the sides, his pointed nose, and forked tail. "He looks fierce, even now," Bob said as we lowered him into the water again.

This fish was pretty badly spent. Directly we put him back he lay over on his side. The danger when a fish is in this condition is that he will drown - yes, literally drown. Exhausted, he will be swept downstream head-first and helpless, the current flooding his gills from the rear, so that he will be unable to breathe by passing water through his mouth and out of his gills. I therefore held him below the surface, head upstream until I felt him beginning to regain his strength. Then he made off for the deeps again, with renewed vigour and a contemptuous flick of his great tail.

It was Bob's turn next. He hooked a 3-pounder and played him very nicely, in view of the fact that he was using a nylon cast of only about 3 lb breaking strain. He might have lost him but for the fact that he remembered to let the rod top take the strain and act as a buffer to the struggles of the fish.

After that we had a long period of silence, so I decided to try a new bait and new tactics.

## *Swimming the Stream*

About 20 yards from us was a deep hole in the river bed where the barbel sometimes lay. This the lock-keeper had pointed out to us as a likely spot. The river swept over the hole in a powerful, smooth glide. This pool, according to our informant, shallowed at its end into a gravel-bottomed shelf - just the place where scared barbel might be lying. The best trick would be to float-fish it, searching it from end to end with the bait dragging the bottom. But it was too far away for a normal cast.

For the first time since we had been fishing together I had reason to use my free-running, or centre-pin reel. These reels are drum reels beautifully balanced so that even a good strong puff of wind will blow them round when the check is off. They are very expensive, but, since they can be used for almost every kind of fishing, they are well worth saving for. A good one can be bought for £2 10s. What are the advantages of a free-running reel? First, you can cast direct from the drum. Secondly, when 'trotting', a strong stream will pull off line on its own.

But don't run away with the idea they are foolproof contraptions or a lazy man's reel. On the contrary, it requires real skill to fish with them. Everyone, I think, should be made to learn to cast accurately with one before graduating to the thread-line reel which I shall be showing you shortly.

But back to the barbel.

I tied on a strong 2x cast, weighting it with six heavy and three medium shot set well down. My float was a cork-covered porcupine quill that would hold up to fourteen shot if necessary; the hook was a No. 10 on to which I had pricked a bunch of four gentles.

The idea was to cast to the top of the pool, check the float until the bait was well on the bottom, and then let the gentles trip along the river bed in a way which barbel are known to find inviting.

I stood up to cast, making the back-swing in the usual manner. As the line flew out, the first tug of float and shot started the drum spinning at an alarming rate. Now, this is why I say the centre-pin is not a lazy man's reel. That first spin of the drum pays off line far faster than it can be taken out. Unless you are careful, therefore, the result will be an 'over-run' on the reel, resulting in a 'bird's nest' that will take ten minutes to sort out.

To prevent this, I kept my finger on the drum of the reel, braking it slightly as it spun during that first split second. Only as the bait got well into the air did I relax my pressure. Then, as the float was just about to hit the water, I slowed and stopped the drum altogether with my finger in order to prevent an over-run at the end of the cast.

It sounds easy, but you try it. It takes more than a morning's fishing to learn the trick properly.

Once the tackle was in the swim, I let the stream revolve the reel, but kept my finger on the check, ready to engage it should the barbel show interest.

At the fifth cast I got a bite, but struck too soon. At the tenth swim down I registered a bite in the identical spot and the float went under. And another barbel, this time one of $3^1/_2$ lb came safely to net.

By ten o'clock the sport is usually over. As this was the case this morning, we decided to put ashore. On the bank we met an angler who had been having some success with 'clay-ball' fishing.

By this method, the fisherman ground-baits with balls of clay into which are rolled worms. The barbel come and prod their sharp snouts into these to pick out the worms.

For Bob's benefit, the angler showed how he baited his hook. First he put on a lob-worm. Then he tied a piece of match-stick on to his cast a foot above the hook, and at right angles to the line. Round this he pressed a largish nob of soft clay containing worm fragments. Finally, he wound the 12 inches of cast down to his hook round the clay-ball and pressed the hook and lob-worm into it, leaving part of the worm sticking out. The whole device he then cast into the swim.

As he explained it, the barbel find the worm sticking out of the clay, pull it out and swallow it without suspecting the hook. Why should they be apprehensive? The balls of ground-bait have already disarmed them.

Bob looked a bit doubtful at these unorthodox tactics, but the angler assured us he had taken two 3-pounders by this method only an hour ago.

As we packed up our tackle, we congratulated ourselves. We had had three nice fish before most people had eaten breakfast, and now we had a splendid appetite for breakfast ourselves.

What is more, from the lock-keeper's cottage was coming a lovely smell of coffee and fried eggs, and I knew him well enough to be sure he would ask us in.

# A Summer Day

*Bernard Venables*

This was back in summer and now, as apples ripen and the tang of September is in the air, the image of it comes back, print-sharp, like something recorded. Momentary details are clear now as then on that summer day, though it was an ordinary enough day, so far as such days are ever ordinary. It was first grey light, and four o'clock, with the dawn chorus starting in separate tentative tinklings of notes, when I came out to take the little road out of the village under the high-hedged banks. This was that odd, still world that comes between dawn and sunrise, when it seems as if human kind is dispossessed, has ceased to be, as if the whole world has been left to the awakening birds and the hares that saunter without fear about the road. The village had the look of blindness that comes then, with blank windows and doors that look sealed-shut. Out of the village, along the little road threading between the fields, the nearly ripened barley was amber and silky under the lightening sky. Then I was out of the by-road labyrinth, going east on the main road, wide and empty, and there was the sun's rim, enormous and red, lifting from the horizon.

It was nearly five o'clock when I came to the bridge, and as I leaned there looking at the river, I noticed as I have so often before, how separate and distinguishable each sound was - blackbird and thrush and wagtail and the sound of the river. It ran very clear under the bridge, not quite silently; we could hear the liquid sibilance of it as it turned and folded over the weed trails and made small swirls through the hanging fronds of the huge weeping willows.

The sun had climbed now, lost its first great redness, but the air was still cool and thin, clear-edged, with that ecstatic smell of early summer morning; there was the curious seeming of a super-reality that is rather dreamlike - the sharp, still, gem-cut precision on everything. In the commoner hours of later day edges are softened. I went down by the small weir and through the gate into the first meadow. The river tossed through the weir gate; the white and cream smother of it ran down fast and broadened and flattened and smoothed away diagonally across towards the far bank. Such water has at all times a fascination and excitement to drug the imagination, and now the invitation of it set me thinking of the barbel that would be waiting where the current slid against the curve of the bank. I thought of them lying restlessly on the gravel, and how the float could dip and slide away when it had run down from under the weir. 'But what sort of a job would you have getting a good fish out there, even if you got it up against the run of the weir,' I thought, looking at the heavy swirl over the stones upon which you would have to stand to net a fish.

The river goes down beautifully for a hundred yards below the weir, with the trees, elms and willows, standing high on our bank and the thrust of current under the other bank. All the way down there the barbel lie, and it has the look of classic barbel water; and, in the warm hours of summer days you can peer down through the mesh of leaves on our bank and see them in the slack, eddying water below, idling concourses of them nudging the roots.

I set up my tackle downstream of the high trees, by the cattle-drink, fumbling a little with the sense of slipping time, because though this world of early summer mornings seems to have the look of a blissful eternity, it is fleeting, too soon declining to ordinary hours that give fish back their caution. The early hours have an innocence, and fish may often come with confidence to the bait; there is an excitement and bewitchment beyond that which is intrinsic to fishing. I began to fish there, captivated by the absorbing pattern of currents where a sidestream came in on the other bank, and I guessed at the pockets of easy water that form within such an amalgamation of currents. Within the meeting of the two streams, I thought, a small shoal probably lay, and I cast the light leger to work from under the bank and from there trundle across to our own bank. 'The chub will be waiting down the easy edge of the faster water,' I thought, and sure enough the first wrench on the rod top came at once when the bait had worked across. But these were only quite small chub, and it was really the splendid barbel run further down that was in my mind. So it so often is; a known objective there may be, but who is to resist the seduction of such water as this was?

But the small chub were persistent, and the game they give soon palls; I went on down, and then the first distant sight of the so-delectable barbel run below the low weir quickened my steps. So far as that may be in that summer trance of early morning I hurried, and noticed how the drench of dew kicked up from my gum boots, catching the sun and making prismatic flashes. And then there, under the high bank, there was the run below the low spill of the weir; and now, though we had hurried, now there was no sense of time. That crystalline water, thrusting down, making a quiet sound through the weed trails, suggesting such a promise of fine fish nosing into the current, cancelled all past, all future. Time, action, event, had stopped; it was sufficient to look at the water, follow and interpret the pattern of its paths of current. The sun glinted on the rumple of water, the smell of warming grass was in the air and the birds sang; moments prolonged into eternity.

I began to fish, and I let the light leger roll with the current, let it insinuate through the weeds, searching under the trails and, as it may be in the early hours, bites came at once. I found no big barbel, but fish seemed to be ranked in every lane through the weeds, not only the barbel, but inevitably the chub, too. They snatched the bait, and if the first snatch was, so to speak, inept, lacking firm skill, you knew it was a small chub and could pull the bait away from it.

If sheer size of the quarry must be the only criterion, this was not great sport; no monstrous barbel came, and it must be doubted if the best chub topped three pounds. But how are you to analyse the pleasures of fishing with a spring balance? In the sunny spangle of sun and air and water there was entire enchantment. And now I noticed that other sounds came from the distant road and village, early sounds of traffic and barking dogs and distance-softened voices. It was seven o'clock, and time had begun again.

The bites were easing away now; the spell was broken. It was nearly the ordinary world of human things, and I moved down again. I went down to the complexity of current where the river begins to broaden, where the heavy weed beds split and divide the river, making fine scours over the gravel. Crouched on the high bank, I noticed that the great willow-herb was opening first flowers in its fat luxuriance of leaf, and how riotously yellow and summer-like the ragwort was along the bank; and there, just before me, was water figwort, and the chiselled facets of its purplish stem had the dull, smooth polish of old furniture, a fine patina. The thistles towered on the bank, with great purple heads.

But the sun was high now, becoming warmer, and here where it fell in strength the fish had become shy. I went down into the spinney of willow and alder, and here the river is wide and a wonderful pattern of quick shallow runs and sudden holes half-hidden by the weed trails. The water glinted and riffled and gurgled faintly past the great beds of ranunculus, smothered now with gold and white blossom. There was a deep privacy here and the swan with her brown brood hissed resentfully; looking backward with gleaming evil eye, she herded her young into the green tunnel of the sidestream.

A great willow stood over the water just downstream, and there, under the bank, the quick run of current fell away abruptly into a hole, with the hole concealed by the heavy mat of floating weed rooted in the shallow above. It was shaded there, and surely in such a place there would be fish to wait out the heat of the day and receive what came borne on the current. And, when the light leger was cast beyond into the open river and allowed to roll round, under, and into the hole, the first bite came at once, wrenching over the rod. I had hoped that barbel might be there, but inevitably there was the big-mouthed gape of a chub, rolling and catching the sun on its bronzy big-scaled flanks. A fine cluster of chub there must have been in that hole, and several of them came before suspicion seized them.

It was high day now, brilliant with sun; it had become drowsy with insect hum through the spinney. The fat bees, heavy-flying, probed the yellow iris flowers; the damsel flies, intense blue or green, hovered and glinted over the water. A warm swoon of summer lay on the river and the spinney. It was time for the fisherman to sit in the shade and conjecture on the currents until evening should send fish foraging again.

## The Nottingham Style

*J. W. Martin*

This fish is a great favourite with Trent and Thames anglers, and when we consider him from all stand-points, it is not to be wondered at, because he is just the chap to fight it out with you to the very last gasp. Powerful, brave, active, vigorous, and handsome, he sometimes puts up a long fight and very often wins at the end of it. Izaak Walton said of him that 'he is so strong that he will often break both rod and line'.

Someone once called my attention to what I consider an extraordinary statement in a book on natural history; it was this: 'When anybody hooks a barbel, the fish always endeavours to strike the line with his tail on purpose to break it'. We generally hook barbel at the bottom of deepish holes, and cannot say with certainty what he is likely to do. I should say he is more likely to ram his old snout into the gravel or sand, or under a stone, or bolt round an old pile of sunken timber in his endeavour to get rid of something that seems to hamper his movements. There is one thing I can say, however, with tolerable certainty, and that is his fighting powers are amazing; that dogged downward boring and his carthorse-like pulls help to prolong the contest beyond the measure of any other fish of equal weight. And after we have, as we think, proved victors in the struggle and he is near the surface apparently played out and done for, as soon as the net is put near him, he suddenly recovers all his lost strength, and bolts off like fury, sometimes to the angler's utter dismay and discomfiture. I know of no fish, not even a lively sea trout, that fights so shy of a landing net. A good rod, reel, and line, in conjunction with fine tackle, however, in the hands of a careful man as described in the previous chapter will circumvent these desperate last rushes of a net-shy barbel.

Once or twice during my Trent career large barbel have broken my rod in these last frantic rushes, but this has been when the rod point was well up, and all the strain under the top ferrule, and I was down on one knee to try and land him, and by some means or other the handle of the reel had caught the edge of my jacket sleeve; generally speaking, I was prepared for Mr Barbel's final effort. The longest fight I ever had with a barbel was in the run of water between the piles of the Midland railway bridge, at foot of the weirs opposite Quibell's Chemical Works, Newark. By some curious twirl of the tackle, the gut and hook had hanked themselves round the root of the tail, and the fish was not hooked at all; that barbel had every chance in his favour, and right well did he stick to his guns. I never had such a job in my life, but being blessed with a big lot of patience, and also anxious to find out what in the world I had hooked on to, I also stuck to my guns, but it was two and a half hours before my big landing net closed the contest, and then it was only a six-pound barbel. What I said in my haste and disappointment had better not be recorded.

In my early days I have known barbel, and many of them, to have been killed on strong water cord and tackle made from twisted copper wire, while the huge ash and lancewood rods weighed as much as three pounds. I handled one one day belonging to a very old angler that appeared to me to be capable of tackling anything, even a sunken gatepost. In the old days everything from rod to hook had to be on the extra strong side; barbel did not get much grace, being hauled ashore without much ceremony.

Nowadays a change has come over things in this respect. Skilled barbel fishermen try to outvie each other in the lightness of their rods, the thinness of their lines, the fineness of their tackle, and the smallness of their hooks; even the barbel themselves have entered into the spirit of the thing, refusing to take a bait at all unless it is presented to them on the finest tackle and the smallest hook, when the cry goes up, "I have got smashed up again." After this has happened two or three times during the day, our angler puts up a set of stouter tackle, but the barbel will have none of it, preferring the small bait, tiny hook, and drawn gut intended for roach and dace. Sometimes when weather and water are favourable a catch may be made by the old-fashioned plan, and even the specimen fish of the year landed on a coarse lobworm and a big gimp hook. One or two of the very best Trent barbel fishermen I know always fish for those fish with a stout roach rod, a fine silk line, a No. 9 Crystal hook, and gut not one whit stouter than 2x drawn. Ground-baiting is the most important item in this branch of fishing.

The barbel is a member of the carp family and is known to science as 'Cyprinus barbus,' or 'Barbus vulgaris.' Naturalists gave him this name on account of the four beards, feelers, or wattles that hang from his mouth, these feelers no doubt being for the purpose of finding his food when he roots his long Roman nose among the sand and gravel on the river's bottom. The top jaw of the fish projects some distance over the bottom one, the mouth being underneath and of a some-what peculiar shape. He is a ground feeder for the most part, frequenting for the greater part of his time the deepest and darkest parts of the river, so this peculiarity of his mouth and the position of the sensitive feelers depending from it is of good service to him. He is a good-looking fish; the colour of his back and partly down his sides is a bright olive-green, tinged with more yellow nearer his white belly, while his large and extra powerful fins, more particularly his pectorals, anal, and ventrals, are edged with a deep purplish red. These combinations of colours give him a very attractive appearance; one thing, however, as a set-off must be noted; look him fair and square in the face and see nothing else, his long downward-pointing nose and his small dark eyes give him a villainous and spiteful look, but this is only a small detail.

Barbel have been denizens of some English rivers for a lengthy period, as is proved by the fact that the fish forms one of the quarterings on the coat of arms of Margaret of Anjou, wife of Henry VI. Scholars and translators agree that the ancient Greeks never mentioned it in any of their writings. The Latin author, Ausonius, who wrote about the fourth century, is the first to mention it. He says, 'And thou, O barbus, harassed by the narrow passes of the winding Saravus, after thou hast descended a river of greater fame, more fully dost exercise spacious swimmings'.

This fish must have been held in high repute during the reign of Queen Elizabeth, for we find that a statute law was passed in her days, 'that anyone taking barbel of less than twelve inches in length should pay twenty shillings', and give up the fish so wrongfully taken, and the net or engine so unlawfully used.' That act has never been repealed, so most likely the anglers of today are liable to the same penalties, but twelve-inch barbel do not weigh as many ounces, so perhaps it would never be put in force, as it is a well known fact that very small barbel are seldom captured with rod and line.

Barbel spawn about the end of May, but do not retire into their regular quarters, deep holes, before July. During June they are sometimes on the streamy shallows, going there after spawning for the purpose of scouring and cleaning themselves; the stream fishermen using the cad-bait for dace very often drop across them and have rare fun on the fine tackle used. They are now in the worst possible condition, being slimy, dirty, and disagreeable. In the old days, when I was out all hours of the day and night, I frequently got evidence of the whereabouts of a huge shoal of barbel. I remember one place in particular, some very wide and streamy shallows not far from a railway bridge that spanned the Trent, this was a specially favoured spot during the darkness of a June night. Those shallows would be literally alive, every now and then there would be a tremendous and long-continued splash, as though a cartload of bricks had been tipped into the river, and this would continue night after night; there was less than two feet of water in that place. A stranger would hardly believe that all that commotion could have been made by fish.

Barbel are not a widely distributed fish like roach, not many rivers having them in abundance, the Thames and the Trent being the principal two in which they are found. These fish seem to thrive more in the warmer latitudes of Europe, being very plentiful in the rivers Danube and Rhine. In the former river, it is said, they reach the great weight of fifty pounds. We have nothing in our rivers like this; the very largest I ever did see and weigh was one caught on a night line by the late Frank Sims, in that stretch of the Trent below Carlton Mill, just before you reach the osier beds; I saw that one pulled out, and it weighed 16 lb 10 oz, a grand fish, even if its end was somewhat unsportsmanlike. It took a big slice of lamprey threaded on a strong wire gorge hook;

it was taken on the 25th of a warm October.

A barbel was preserved at Newark that exceeded fourteen pounds; this was fairly landed on rod and line. I once saw and handled seven that went nearly forty-three pounds, and I don't think there was half a pound difference in weight between any of them. Now and again at rare intervals some lucky angler gets a tremendous catch of barbel. A friend of mine at Newark, on the Trent, only two or three years ago, got ninety-seven in one day, and about three hundred in the week's fishing; another Newark man got no less than one hundred and twenty-three in a single day. And so we look back over the newspaper reports and find well-known Thames anglers who have had occasionally catches of barbel that border on the marvellous. My own record was got on the Berkshire Kennet, and numbered thirty-three all told. There are a few famous swims down the Lower Trent where the barbel run a good average size; I had five one day going twenty-six pounds, taken on boiled greaves, old cheese, and some of Charlie Hudson's patent puddings used as ground-baits.

Another deep swim, just above the bream hole at Dunham Dubbs nearly opposite the 'Shuttle Door', that Charlie and I baited up for two or three days, yielded three barbel only, but every one went from seven to eight pounds each; lobworms were the bait that evening. Taking things on the whole, barbel fishing is disappointing to gauge it by actual results, but it is enjoyable. I found that in the majority of swims we got three fish under three pounds to one over that figure, some swims were worse in this respect than others; some swims again, like the celebrated Scotchman's Hole at Marnham, or the Hully Gully at Averham, or the weir pool at the bottom locks, or the famous Putty Nob at Girton, occasionally gave us a 'tonker', and sometimes a broken tackle. Barbel fishing was a sport that I was particularly fond of. I remember once during a slack time at the works, or a holiday, going on foot seven miles each way every morning and night for a week, fishing till nine o'clock each night, and at them next morning by noon or before, and only getting fish on the close of the last day, just at sundown. I legered, long-corked, and floated; never once did I relax my efforts; never ceased from tiddling the clipped-up worms in. Five times I trudged home with an empty creel, but that last night I floated the swim till I could not see the float, and got fish; then I legered and got them, finally finishing up with twelve fish going, as near as nothing, forty pounds when weighed in, largest four and a quarter pounds. I consider that is about an average experience, more blanks than bags, but still I kept going, year after year, week by week, and never considered it time wasted. Did not the late Tom Bentley and I tramp to Stoke Park, Notts, one day a week for five weeks running, carrying a thousand lobs with us every time, and fished one of the most famous barbel swims on that famous river, and only got fish twice? Once we had a bag of thirteen and the other time only five, and not one fish exceeded three pounds.

Andrew Broughton, Tommy Sunman, Frank Sims, Charlie Hudson, and other well-known barbel fishermen have been with me, and we have tried all we knew; we have seen the fish hurl themselves from the water time and again, all down a celebrated stretch; have coaxed them with all sorts of things, and blanks have been more numerous than bags; but still, as a sport it ranks among the highest class, and whether you sit on a basket and leger in the depths of a weir hole, or float heavy current on a glorious summer's evening, it is an experience never to be forgotten, whether the bag is heavy or whether it is light.

One of my dear old friends used to say that an angler was not worth his salt unless he could kill a six-pound barbel on a 2x drawn gut tackle. I may say that I have killed them nearly that weight on even finer than that when I have been dacing down the streams with a scrap of greaves or a bunch of gentles on the hook. I hardly care to recommend this fineness in a general way, but I am a user and an advocate of fine tackle; I generally use the same tackle for barbel as I use for chub, and if water is open and plenty of sea room no danger need be feared. Some of the men down the Lower Trent use queer baits now and again for barbel; fish have been caught on strips of raw lean beef, strips of cooked lean ham, bits of Yorkshire pudding, pieces of tripe, even cockles, mussels, whelks, and tiny sand eels have been utilised with occasional success. And why not! Sometimes a fish may be attracted by a monstrosity that looks like nothing else on the banks or in the water, and so in a tidal water like the Lower Trent, why not try anything that takes the fancy? In a river in which the water ebbs and flows some feet each way twice a day there is no telling what may be attractive to these hunting barbel.

In an ordinary barbel river the haunts of these fish are not very difficult to find if the eyes are kept open; especially during August they will be seen leaping from the water. These fish are troubled with external parasites, and they frequently leap in order, I dare say, to rid themselves of the nuisance. If this leaping is noticed and it is pretty well kept up all down a good stretch of water, you can conclude that a very considerable shoal has taken possession of that run of water.

One place more than another they delight in is under and about the woodwork of an old bridge, providing there is seven or eight feet of water there; and also you are certain to find them in or near the rushing, tumbling waters of a weir hole, and also in a very heavy deep stream, as their powerful fins enable them to stem the strongest current. Backwaters and side streams with old posts and sunken trees in them that form deep eddies and good cover are almost sure finds, while the deep runs over the rocks and boulders that go down into the stream should not be neglected. A hollow clay bank under which a big current glides and then gurgles round like an umbrella swim is also a good place, or a deep hole or eddy close to an abrupt bend in the river. Many of these bends have the water rushing hard under the bank, washing out in course of time a shelf, and then the stream sets out again towards the centre of the river, leaving all sorts of curls and eddies in its track. The nature of a place like this is all in favour of barbel being found in it, as natural and artificial food would be swept under the bank and gradually work down into those eddying curls and runs.

Barbel are good fish on the fine tackle of a Nottingham angler, and look well in a glass case if they go anything over ten pounds, and that is about all you can say for them. Charley Hudson's granddaughter who could cook freshwater fish with anybody, confessed herself beaten with barbel. We did try once or twice when I was down there to make something of one, but the woolly, watery flesh full of small and irritating bones was too much for us, and I remember we made a good veal stuffing and put several rolls of beautiful crisp bacon on small skewers on him, and basted him well. The stuffing and bacon were far away the best part of that banquet; in fact, our cook for the time being said she had made the stuffing extra good and a plentiful supply of it; the bacon, together with a dish of vegetables made an excellent substitute for a dinner. I give you my experience; anglers can have them cooked if they like, but I would sooner have a good perch, or a dish of freshwater flounders.

In concluding this chapter I may say that nowadays barbel fishing is by no means a certainty. Thirty-five or more years ago they were nearly always 'on' during August and September, more or less; anyhow, we could generally get from one to four or five fish during the evening after tea, and once now and again a very decent bag was had. As a sport when they are 'on' it is grand; I know of nothing to beat it.

## Walking Away from the Thames

*John Ginifer*

I know exactly why it ended that dark, dank Friday evening, in late October. Walking heavily, along the narrow garden path, leading away from Potts Stream, a tributary of the Thames, known to some for its huge barbel, I needed to reach my parked car. Behind me, an extraordinary pool flowed quietly, within me there was turmoil.

This story unwinds from my boyhood, when a fishing uncle sent a copy of Patrick Chalmers' wickedly evocative, *At the Tail of the Weir.* Nothing else would do, until he arranged a meeting with the best fisherman who ever fished the Thames, A. E. Hobbs. This living legend showed me his collection of glass cases, enclosing wonderful fishes, especially huge and beautiful trout which, beyond all others, he had caught in profusion. He mentioned how he had tipped lock-keepers to pinpoint large Thames trout that showed around their weirs and locks. How each year, he and others stocked the weirs and selected main stretches with farm-reared trout. But sole blow to my visit, he discouraged me from attempting to trout fish the Thames, because of the difficulty I would have in visiting it frequently. Rather, I should try for barbel, which he would initiate by fixing up a few hours in the boat of the Thames professional, J. L. Webb.

I knew of Mr Webb, whose compelling writings on barbel, I had devoured in "BB's" *The Fisherman's Bedside Book*. Hobbs carefully prepared me as to how I should react to this rough but trusty character, whose language, dress and presence were somewhat unusual for a lad used to grammar school teachers and a meticulous mother. I survived a morning with this character: learning to catch and eat gudgeon; becoming familiar with a wide range of oaths, most of which I failed to understand; but best of all, being inspired by his absolute conviction that barbel grow to 20 lb, and plenty more, in the Thames and Kennet. A seed was sown.

Fifteen years passed before I took up Webb's astute advice and fished the shallow, clear and gravelly reaches downstream of Aldermaston, where I had the immense advantage of studying the shoals of barbel that thrived there. To advance beyond competence in fishing it is vital to understand the nature, habits and environment of your quarry. By comparison, the acquisition of appropriate tackle and technique is child's play.

In five crowded years, I learnt a great deal about the movements and feeding habits of Kennet barbel, and perhaps most importantly to seek the largest fish in level swims, from 8-10 feet deep, preferably those not commonly known to hold fish. Towards the bottom of the Reading AC stretch there is a deep hole, with a gravelly bottom and steady current - the very spot for big fish. It is a long walk and, when reached, the heavily overgrown bank and dark wood give off a sombre, threatening feel. Not once did I find evidence of other fishermen and, unusually, the place gave me the creeps. First, it produced a specimen of 9 lb 11 oz, easily the best I have caught from the Kennet. Then, catastrophically and sadly, it became the death place of a young local man I knew, who was found shot by his own gun. The hole went silent - time to move to the Thames.

Where to start? I considered the spot opposite to the third meadow below The French Horn at Sonning, where Webb had landed his 12-pounder. I knew too about the heaviest Thames barbel of 14 lb 6 oz caught in 1888 by T. Wheeler at lovely Moseley; and of the 14 lb 4 oz one, landed by P. Jones at Radcot

Bridge in 1908. My problem was solved by that master Thames fisherman of today, Peter Stone, who took me to a deceptively productive stream, in the centre of Oxford called Potts, where double-figure barbel could be found. How generous and typically unselfish of Peter, to whom I owe a great debt.

Potts barbel were magnificent specimens, with flanks coloured dark olive and brown, overlaced with gold. Their thick girth and very heavy shoulders made them significantly heavier than Avon fish of the same length. They were immensely strong and very suspicious of baits. For three years, a string of double-figure barbel rewarded my best efforts, with seven between 10 and 11 lb, until finally my dearly missed friend, Gwynn Williams, landed one over 12 lb. This fish opened my eyes. I had pointed out to him that an upstream cast would place his bait between the much-pounded pool where he was fishing, and a smaller, untouched one above, to which a high garden fence barred access. Within hours of fishing this fresh swim, he caught his best barbel. The penny dropped - hunt, don't trap.

I devoted the first two weeks of my summer holidays, canoeing the main river and connecting side-streams, around Oxford, searching for swims that met the golden barbel criteria: 8–10 feet deep, with a level, hard bottom and steady current. I have a lovely list of these runs, which to this day sets me dreaming. Finally, I took my canoe to Potts stream, paddling past the fence where Gwynn had caught his biggest barbel. Barely a hundred yards below the main road, which marks the top of Potts, there came a deep, steady pool.

In full view, three immense fish finned quietly in the shallow tail of this run. The smallest I estimated between 13 and 14 lb.; the next, alongside it, was well over 14 lb, probably 15–16 lb; the largest, fanning giant pectorals, was simply massive - as long as a 20 lb salmon I once caught, but surely thicker. I watched fascinated, holding steady the canoe with all the skill I could muster, as coolly as possible estimating their size. No matter how objectively I tried to reduce their estimated weights, they remained from a little below 14 lb to at least 20. I sat stock-still, watching - enchanted.

As if divining my presence, this tremendous leash of giants grew restless, giving early signs of slipping to the opaque depths above. I could not resist introducing myself to my new opponents, so with rock steady strokes, I whispered the canoe towards them, reaching about seven yards from a handshake, before they shadowed out of sight. Imagine that fantastic experience!

Within two evenings, unique permission was wheedled from the baker, whose garden flanked the left bank of the coveted pool. As the right bank was unfishable, I was in virgin territory - no wonder that magnificent trio had felt safe in the shallow tail.

I took up a place half way down the pool and, with light fading fast, made my first cast a little upstream, handing the rod to Zena, while I ground-baited the head of the pool. Quietly and deliberately, I tossed in weighted, hook-sized pieces of black pudding, which were judged to settle where the pool first deepened, or at most trundle a little way downstream. As I pussy-footed back to my fishing rod, the line gently shook, slowly tightened, and as I made a huge bound towards it, Zena struck home the hook, gasping at its first, fierce lunge and my hand desperately retrieving my rod!

This immensely strong fish was not a runner, it kept low and refused to budge. When a barbel sets its pectorals and hugs the bottom, its resistance to movement is extraordinary, yet it is actually resting. I always try to outmanœuvre powerful fish, bringing them to net before they are exhausted; this barbel intended to turn the tables on me. I quietly shifted my position, wound down the rod tip and steadily increased the strain, bending deeply into the butt of the Hunter rod, until the line went stretchy. Slowly at first, then with frightening ease, it fled downstream into the tail of the pool, where two days previously I had first spotted it. With barely a pause, it shot out of the tail, downstream into a shallow run that led to a small and very snaggy pool, through which I had had difficulty canoeing.

As I slackened the pressure, it settled somewhere below, allowing that old salmon fisherman's trick of walking it upstream, back to safety. It followed like a lamb, through the glassy tail of my pool and into the long, quiet eddy that gently spun on my side of the pool. I decided the fight would end here and as it attempted to regain the mid-currents, I swung my rod this way and that, virtually tricking it into the waiting net. As the net was lifted, too late it exploded into action, as if at last realising it had capitulated with the fight hardly begun. Drenched, I looked down at the junior member of the three gods, weighing just over 13½ lb. Gently held in the eddy, to regain its full composure, there could be no question as to its identity - it was the fish I had judged, just below 14 lb. I released the third largest barbel known to have been caught in the Thames.

It is hard to take in such riches but at last I recognised what had been driving me these past twenty years. Rather than a British record fish, I longed to catch a master barbel, confirming as Hobbs and Webb had always maintained, Thames barbel grow to 20 lb and plenty more. Without quite realising it, I had fallen under the spell of this historic river, its fantastic fish and the characters that haunt it yet.

Time was compressing events. As I walked down the garden path, leading to Potts paradise that warm, moist Friday evening, in late October, I knew it could well be my last chance that year, for much colder weather was forecast. Not only that, three months later I was due to start a research thesis at the University of Newcastle-upon-Tyne, following which I might be employed anywhere in the UK. Worse still, in the year and a half since I had discovered this fabulous pool, the Thames was increasingly showing the ill effects of land drainage, motorised boats, abstraction and agricultural pollution. Potts was slowly silting up; beds of rushes were narrowing its main channel; crayfish no longer tweaked the bait; weed life and abundant shrimps were drastically reduced; the water had a tired look. How much longer could it provide the pristine habitat that nurtured these extraordinary barbel?

Concentrating on the task in hand, I lobbed upstream - an easy cast to the head of the pool, feeling the bait and swan-shot leger softly settle on the hard riverbed. I love the sense and feel of Oxford just before Guy Fawkes night, associating it with darkening evenings, the crack of a premature firework and that rotting, smoky smell of burning autumn leaves and garden cuttings. In the diffuse urban half-light I could clearly see the rod, with the wet curve of line waiting patiently for the soft touch of a big barbel. With line gently held between the fingertips, as delicately as undoing strange buttons in the dark, it was hard to believe on such a warm, still night that a barbel could fail to keep its appointment.

No two bites are alike but the one that set me alight was tantalisingly slow. First the merest tremble, which was within a whisker of triggering a premature re-action; then a gentle lift that hardly changed the line's lazy curve; finally a slow, slackening fall of line that brought an instant strike and violent reaction. An immense force simply shifted from the head of the pool to its tail, without a hint of tug or thump - one sudden, smooth, unstoppable sweep of power, that ripped line off a screaming reel. It stopped as violently as it started, apparently with no intention of leaving the pool.

I was intimidated by the suddenness and sheer force of this fish but cruel experience had taught me the importance of exerting some authority over a power-ful fish, for to give it its head in such cramped circumstances is almost to guarantee its escape.

I slipped downstream until almost opposite the hooked barbel, then swung the rod towards me, momentarily moving it slightly off balance. Its reaction left no possible doubt as to its size, for the responding surge plunged down the rod tip, in an instant forcing a tortured reel to give twenty yards of line. Of its own accord, it then crossed the pool, to finish upstream of me, but in the eddy on my side, therefore offering a wonderful opportunity to pressurise it.

No time for faint hearts, I simply leant into the rod, determined not to give an inch of line, without the fish paying for it. For a moment, we grappled as equals. Gradually it increased its resistance, sounding my strength, until no longer could I restrain its immense power. I felt the uncanny sensation of knowing this huge creature. Again, the rod plunged down almost to the water before the reel released the tension, but the sound of the Mitchell reel had changed from its usual sharp, mechanical whine to crunchy jerks. Had I sand or grit in it? Instinctively, I thrust the reel under the surface to gain some lubrication. This worked, for again that ruthless flow of power took the barbel across the pool, deep, deep down to where I had first hooked it. As if to test my reactions, the barbel moved down the opposite side of the pool, giving me the chance to exert fierce side-strain, which curved its path towards the eddy on my side. Anticipating a sudden reaction, I frantically cupped water over my rasping reel and braced myself for the surge that would crush me.

What followed was inevitable, yet almost bizarre. The rod bent deeply, with the reel jerking and scraping a terrible tune; I plunged bankside into the soft, silted reed-bed, to gain precious yards, for by now the force on the line was crippling. With a final screech, the Mitchell jammed tight and the line broke at the top ring like a gunshot, leaving a faint puff of vapour drifting on the evening air. For the briefest moment, the unconnected line lay like a snake on the surface before slithering into the deeps, leaving me utterly alone.

I heard my pleadings softly echo from the walls and fences of Oxford: "Oh. No. No. No."

Walking heavily, along the narrow garden path, leading away from Potts Stream, that dark, dank Friday evening in late October, I had reached the end of a long quest. It was a journey travelled before me, by those supreme fishermen, Hobbs and Webb, both of whom had hooked monster barbel they were not to bring to net. I turned the ignition switch and left the Thames behind me.

# Acknowledgements

'The Avon at Ibsley', previously unpublished, copyright Chris Yates.

'The Middle Avon' by Dick Walker from *The Fighting Barbel* edited by Peter Wheat (Benn, 1967), reproduced by kind permission of Peter Wheat.

'The House Pool' from *Favourite Swims* by Fred J. Taylor (1961), reproduced by kind permission of Fred J. Taylor.

'Weir-pools, Worms, Tea and Barbel', from *Coarse Fishing* by H. T. Sheringham, (A & C Black, 1912).

'A Midnight Battle with a Monster Barbel' by J. L. Webb from *The Fisherman's Bedside Book*, edited by "BB", Eyre and Spottiswood, 1945.

'The Upper Thames', by John Ginifer, from *The Fighting Barbel* edited by Peter Wheat (Benn, 1967), reproduced by kind permission of Peter Wheat.

'Fishing for Barbel' by Michael Shephard, from *Come and Fish*, (Museum Press, 1952).

'The Barbel' by Patrick Chalmers, from *At the Tail of the Weir* (Philip Allan, 1932).

'The Barbel Swim' by Peter Wheat, from *The Fighting Barbel* edited by Peter Wheat (Benn, 1967), reproduced by kind permission of Peter Wheat.

'The Barbel and how to Bait for Him' by Philip Geen, from *What I Have Seen While Fishing and How I Have Caught My Fish* (T. Fisher Unwin, London. 1905).

'No Need to Lie' by Dick Walker from *No Need to Lie* (1964), reproduced by kind permission of Pat Walker.

'The Tiger of the Weir pool' by Colin Willock, from *Come Fishing with Me* (Frederick Muller, 1952), reproduced by kind permission of Colin Willock.

'A Summer Day' by Bernard Venables, first published in Creel magazine (September 1964), and reproduced with the kind permission of Bernard Venables.

'The Nottingham Style' by J. W. Martin, from *Coarse Fish Angling* (W. Brendon & Son Plymouth, 1900).

'Walking Away from the Thames', by John Ginifer, written especially for this collection and reproduced with the permission of the author.

*The publishers have made every effort to contact the copyright holders but if any have been inadvertently overlooked they should contact the publishers immediately.*